Teaching and counselling

Teaching and counselling
Pastoral care in primary and secondary schools

David Galloway

Longman London and New York

Longman Group Limited
Longman House,
Burnt Mill, Harlow, Essex, UK

Published in the United States of America
by Longman Inc., New York

© *David Galloway 1981*

First published 1981

British Library Cataloguing in Publication Data

Galloway, David
  Teaching and counselling.
  1. Personnel service in education -
  Great Britain — Case studies
  I. Title
  371.4'0941   LB1027.5   79-41821

  ISBN 0-582-48987-3

Printed in England by M\^cCorquodale (Newton) Ltd., Newton-le-Willows, Lancashire.

Contents

Disclaimers

The views expressed in this book are the author's own and should not be taken to represent those of his present or previous employers.

The people and schools described in the case histories in this book are fictitious and any resemblance to people living or dead is entirely coincidental.

PART I
Introduction

Teaching and counselling: A personal view

Some people regard counselling as a rather esoteric activity applied by specialists to pupils with problems; others regard counselling as a normal part of the day-to-day activities of all teachers with responsibility for guidance and pastoral care. Where the basic unit of pastoral care is the form tutor, this will involve most teachers in the school. The first view is in danger of enveloping an essentially human activity in a pseudo-psychological mystique. The second is in danger of placing a respectable label on an old-fashioned lecture.

In the title of this book, counselling does not necessarily imply face-to-face discussion between teacher and child. It implies a teacher's careful assessment of the child's needs and the ways in which the school can meet those needs. The assessment and possible solutions are based on systematic observation, on discussion between teachers, and on interviews with the child himself and with his parents. Most of the children described in the following case histories have personal problems. They all present their teachers with problems, so they are disturbing even if they are not disturbed.

To say that a child is disturbing to his teachers or to other pupils implies an interaction between him and them. He may be disturbing because of his aggressive, attention-seeking or unpredictably disruptive behaviour; on the other hand, he may be disturbing because of his tense, nervous or withdrawn manner. To argue that the problem resides entirely in the child or his family is misleading and undervalues the school's and the teacher's own significance in the child's life. Some children can undoubtedly benefit from personal counselling. It is a central thesis of this book, however, that personal counselling is not always appropriate and is seldom, if ever, effective unless combined with a conscious attempt to deal with the problem where it occurs − in the classroom or the playground.

This view of counselling extends far beyond an adult's therapeutic sessions with a child. It includes the assessment and modification of teaching methods, pastoral responsibilities, and policy on discipline, where these are found to contribute to the problems about which the school, and perhaps the child, are complaining. A valid objection might be that such a definition of counselling is indistinguishable from pastoral care with problem pupils. This is probably true. The point, though, is that neither counselling nor pastoral care can operate successfully except as an integral part of the school's educational aims and objectives.

The title: *Teaching and counselling* was preferred to *Teaching and pastoral care* in order to direct attention more specifically to the connection between the organisation and practice of classroom teaching and the needs of individual children. To put the same point in a different way, counselling implies work with individuals, while pastoral care may imply a system of care and guidance.

Pastoral care and the myth of never-ending toil [1]

The head of a large Leeds comprehensive school has likened pastoral care to the labour of Sisyphus (Spooner 1979). In Greek mythology, Sisyphus was father of Odysseus. As punishment for his wickedness during life in this world, in the underworld the Gods made him roll a heavy boulder to the top of a hill; at the top it would roll down again, whereupon Sisyphus had to push it up again . . . and so on for the rest of eternity. "When one steps back and surveys the educational scene", Spooner comments, "one frequently finds this unlikely phenomenon actually taking place. Living in a world to all intents and purposes isolated from reality, teachers present a daily ration of 'education' to some boys and girls whose living conditions destroy it."

Parkinson's Law offers another way of looking at the same problem, or at least a similar one. Work expands in proportion to the time available for it. Never before have teachers been so aware of the social and psychological difficulties facing their pupils. Never before have so many teachers had posts of special responsibility for discipline and/or pastoral care. A teacher with specific responsibility either for discipline or for pastoral care may not go out of his way to find problems. Yet both the formal organisation and the informal ethos of the school can conspire to ensure that problems find him.

For example, the year tutor's job description often emphasises responsibilities such as investigating instances of under-achievement, counselling children with behavioural or emotional problems, liaising with outside agencies about pupils with special needs, following up cases of poor attendance, investigating and dealing with children who have been disruptive in class, and so on. A year tutor or head of house who takes these seriously is in some danger of becoming a cross between an unqualified social worker and a volunteer in the citizens' advice bureau. At best he will persuade his colleagues not to refer any but the most intransigent problems to him, so that he may then refer them to the head or to appropriate outside agencies. At worst, he will work himself to an early coronary, losing in the process much of his credibility as a teacher.

The argument is not that cases of poor attendance, disruptive behaviour, poor scholastic achievement, and so on, should not be carefully investigated. Satisfactory pastoral care depends, as a Minister in the first Thatcher government once said of truancy, "on constant if not eternal vigilance" (Boyson, 1974).

There are three recurring themes in this book. The first is that counselling and pastoral care is primarily about a child's achievements and social adjustment *at school*. Concern about his problems at home is secondary to this. Unfortu-

1 The title of the article by Spooner (1979)

nately, conscientious and sensitive teachers, not to mention education welfare officers and educational psychologists, who start looking for problems at home generally find them. It is then a short step to excusing the child's poor behaviour, progress or attendance. This is a recipe for inertia. As Spooner says, "You do not, when children find food difficult to digest, excuse them from eating."

It is worth pursuing the implications of the easy trap of believing that to understand all is to forgive all. It loses sight of the primary aims in a child's pastoral care, namely: (i) to help his teachers meet his educational needs more appropriately, and (ii) to help the child himself find constructive solutions to his problems of social adjustment. Worse, it removes any incentive to examine ways in which the school's own organisation and methods may exacerbate the child's problem. Looking for causes in the child, his family or his neighbourhood reduces anxiety in the short run. In the long run it increases frustration and anxiety in at least two ways: (i) in practice there is not always much that can be done about the problems that are unearthed; (ii) teachers' morale is reduced by a feeling of helplessness in the face of their pupils' overwhelming social problems, and as their morale sinks so do their expectations.

The second recurring theme in the case histories that follow is that schools can — and frequently do — go some way to compensate for the effects of stress that originate outside school. Using knowledge of difficulties at home to provide a more satisfactory education for the child at school is one of the most critical, but least developed, aspects of counselling and pastoral care. The other side of this particular coin is that a good deal of counselling is self-induced in the sense that many problems referred to year tutors or counsellors are the product, at least in part, of school organisation and classroom practice.

There are two responses to these children. One is to call in outside agencies to identify the problems of the child and his family that have caused the failure or the disturbance. If these problems prove intractable, the child can be referred to an educational psychologist in his capacity as Special Schools Removals Officer. The other possible response is to identify the problems of the child or his family in order to examine the possible ways in which his experience at school contributes to or reduces these problems.

The third recurring theme throughout the book is that pastoral care cannot be divorced from good teaching. The year tutor or head of house who expects — or is expected — to deal with routine pastoral or disciplinary matters himself is doomed to failure. In a comprehensive school he will probably be responsible for between 120 and 400 children, depending on the size of the school. The crude naïvety of the idea that one person, or even two if he has an assistant, can cope adequately with the routine pastoral care of this number of pupils is widely, if not universally recognised. Yet this recognition is by no means always reflected in a well-developed form tutor system.

In primary schools the class teacher has the same pastoral responsibilities as the secondary school form tutor and so this does not apply. In secondary schools, though, each child may be taught by as many as a dozen teachers in the course of the week. Normally none of these teachers have a general responsibility for monitoring his overall educational progress and social adjustment. None of them have the specific responsibility of knowing him well as an individual. The only person who can theoretically fulfil these responsibilities is the class tutor, yet in practice he may find himself unable to do so. This can happen because year tutors are seen as having personal responsibility for pastoral care, rather than responsibility for co-ordinating the pastoral care of a team of form tutors. It can also happen because form tutors only stay with their forms for one year, or two at the most. It can happen because form tutors are given inadequate time to do anything with their form except fill in the attendance register.

Needless to say, the view that pastoral care is a normal and necessary part of good teaching also has implications for the organisation and content of the school's curriculum. Some of the case histories in Parts II and III identify difficulties that can arise from policy decisions on curriculum organisation. The argument is not that the policy decisions were wrong; they may indeed have been the best possible decisions for the majority of children in the light of the teachers' experience and the school's resources at the time they were made. The argument is rather that if a particular form of organisation has proved unsuccessful for a particular child, it is helpful to be clear about the reasons why before deciding that no change is possible or desirable.

The dilemma of counselling and pastoral care

When the school leaving age was raised to fifteen in 1947 there were few, if any, counsellors in schools; few, if any, teachers had salaried posts with special responsibility for pastoral care. In 1950 less than 600 pupils were receiving their education in special schools for the maladjusted, and only just over 15,000 in special schools for the ESN(M). By 1976 over 13,600 were receiving education in schools for the maladjusted and over 53,700 in schools for the ESN(M) (D.E.S., 1977). In addition, several universities had established courses in counselling for experienced teachers, and virtually all secondary schools had established some sort of formal pastoral care system.

Parallel with these developments, there has grown up what Reynolds and Murgatroyd (1977) call "a veritable army of members of the 'helping professions'". This "veritable army" consists of education welfare officers – increasingly known as education social workers – educational psychologists, voluntary agencies such as Family Service Units and the N.S.P.C.C., school medical officers and school nurses, local education authority advisers, careers officers, and so on. These services may have developed in response to a perceived need, but it is not at all clear that they have developed in response to an increase in the prevalence of problems facing children or their families.

Surveys of the prevalence of learning difficulties and behaviour problems have failed to establish any significant changes over time (Galloway and Goodwin, 1979). There are significant regional variations, with more problems in inner-city areas (Rutter et al, 1975), but there is general agreement, both before and since the Second World War, on the numbers of children with special needs. This general agreement led the Warnock Committee to conclude that one child in six might require some form of special education at any one time, and one child in five at some stage in his school career (D.E.S., 1978).

The increase in services has, of course, followed increasing recognition of the difficulties facing a large number of children. What is disappointing is the widespread lack of agreement that these children's needs are now being met more satisfactorily than before the development of pastoral and external support services. The achievements of special schools for the ESN(M) and the maladjusted have been called into question (Osterling, 1967; Galloway and Goodwin, 1979). Remedial teaching has been shown to have short-term effects, yet in the long term this benefit is often lost through inadequate follow-up (Sampson, 1975; Cashdan and Pumfrey, 1969). Encouraging results have been claimed from the introduction of counsellors and social workers into schools (Rose and Marshall, 1974), but without adequate replication the implications have not been reflected in general policy or practice.

A way out of the dilemma

The role of outside agencies   The dilemma of counselling and pastoral care lies in the huge increase in manpower and services with no corresponding reduction in the quantity, nor in the severity, of the problems which teachers feel they face. The way out of the dilemma lies in a critical analysis of the underlying aims of counselling and pastoral services, and of their place in a broader educational philosophy and practice. In this connection it is important to look carefully at the role of the external support services as well as at that of the school's own staff.

Understandably, both educational, medical and social work support services have been child and family orientated. The general procedure has been for schools to define the problem as they see it, and for the educational psychologist, social worker, child psychiatrist, or school medical officer to interview the child and his parents in order to throw light on the school's problem. Occasionally they even offer the child and/or his parents something called treatment in the hope that it will cure the school's problem. Naturally, they are also concerned with helping the family, but it is as well to be clear about the initial reason for referral and about the pressure which the school as referring agent can continue to exert on the services concerned.

This model of outside agencies as experts in problem solving could perhaps be acceptable if they did in fact have expertise in solving the sort of problems which schools face. Their frequent failure to solve, or even to ameliorate, the problems referred to them generates frustration and cynicism in teachers. What is worse, their "expert" status encourages teachers themselves to adopt a similar model, looking for the cause of problems in the child or his family, rather than in the pattern of the child's success and failure at school. The outsider's expert status is not seriously undermined by his frequently demonstrable lack of expertise. This is partly because he is often able to speak with the voice of authority and may hold the key to scarce resources such as special school places; more important, the mere fact of referral can reduce anxiety by engendering a feeling of "we've done what we can; now it's up to them."

The status of outside expert is helpful neither to the "experts" themselves nor to the teachers responsible for counselling, pastoral care and remedial education within the school. It is a model which has been severely attacked by a number of educational psychologists (Gillham, 1978), many of whom are developing a new relationship with schools as equal partners.

The Warnock Report spoke of parents as partners (D.E.S., 1978). Equally important is the need for teachers and outside agencies to work with parents and with each other as partners in meeting the child's needs at school. A cynic might say that if all partners are equal, some are more equal than others. Such a view misses the point that if a child is to be helped, the adults who can help him will be the adults with whom he spends most of his time, namely his parents and his teachers. The outsider's role is to bring independent ideas to bear on the problem, supported, hopefully, by his own specialist knowledge and experience. The point of the specialist knowledge and experience, however, is not to explain the problem so much as to help the teachers in their own analysis of ways in which the school itself may have contributed to the problem and of possible ways to reduce it.

Analysing problem situations   Recognising that the school may contribute to the problem is much easier in theory than in practice. Understanding how a broken home, an alcoholic parent, or a multiply-handicapped sibling may affect the child's concentration and association with "undesirable" elements is easier, for example, than understanding how the school's system of pastoral care and remedial education contribute to the behaviour about which the school itself is complaining. There are two distinct issues:

(*i*) Most people have a fairly clear, though often idealised, idea of what they consider "normal" family life. Thus, most teachers would consider broken homes, physical or psychiatric illness, or a parent's criminal record as "abnormal" and, hence, as possible explanations for deviant behaviour or poor progress at school. The fact that the people labelled in this way might have a quite different conception of normality is not strictly relevant at the moment.

(*ii*) In school there is no idealised norm. Teachers argue fiercely both about the aims of education and about the most suitable ways to achieve them. At national level the controversy over special education and, in a few die-hard areas, over comprehensive re-organisation are good examples. At staff room level, controversy abounds on the merits of vertical or horizontal pastoral groups, the need for behavioural units for problem pupils, full-time remedial classes versus part-time withdrawal groups, mixed-ability teaching versus setting or banding, and so on.

A point which is made in several of the case histories in Parts II and III is that there is no correct answer. The quality of education is determined by individuals, not by theory. Theoretically, for example, a "remedial" class of fifteen or twenty of the slowest and most difficult pupils in their final two years at a large primary school is almost a contradiction in terms. How can a teacher *remedy* individual problems in a class that size? Children learn from each other, so if you put your problems together you can only increase them. The needs of slow learning children are quite different from those of the disruptive or maladjusted.

All of these arguments are valid in theory, yet may sometimes be invalidated by circumstances in a particular school. Some primary school teachers, for example, enjoy the challenge of teaching children with learning and behavioural problems, and have a long record of success with them. These teachers are not

7

always willing to take withdrawal groups, since this would mean giving up the satisfaction that comes from having a class of their own and observing their pupils' progress over the year. The head may then have a choice between pressuring them to do something against their wishes, or giving them a class of children with problems.

School policy has to be determined in the light of the available teaching skills and material resources. Theory and practice illuminate each other, but the eventual decision must be pragmatic. An almost invariable characteristic of problem children, however, is that they challenge the correctness of pragmatic decisions. The slow-learning or retarded child's failure to make progress in reading, questions the methods and reading schemes which have been used to teach him. The disturbing child questions the quality — and even the legitimacy — of the teacher's authority (Hargreaves, 1967; Hargreaves *et al.*, 1975).

Especially in the younger age groups, most children will happily conform to any educational diet they are given, however dreadful. It is difficult, for example, to imagine anything more artificial linguistically, less likely to stimulate children's imagination, and further removed from their own reality, than the awful jerk-jerk chatter of the synthetic characters in the most widely used reading schemes in infant schools (Bugler, 1976). Yet most children accept these books without question. They accept them partly because of their teachers' skill in arousing their interest in material which is intrinsically devoid of interest, but partly also because of their own sense of security in any teacher-directed task at which they can achieve success.

The same principles apply in secondary schools, though in this age group pupils become increasingly critical of what the school is offering them. If unauthorised absentee figures are any guide, they opt out in increasing numbers as they grow older (Galloway, 1976). Whether we are talking about truants, disruptive pupils or pupils who fail to make educational progress, it remains true that they identify the weaknesses in the school's facilities. Indeed, the only other group of children who help teachers to recognise their own limitations are the gifted. They too challenge the system — in a different way.

Using the case histories

Purpose and scope   Part II contains nine pairs of case histories set in primary schools, and Part III nine pairs set in secondary schools. Each pair consists of a "case" history describing some aspect of the school's pastoral, remedial or general educational organisation, followed by a case history of a child at the school. The school histories concentrate on policy matters that arise almost annually in most average-sized or large schools.

The emphasis is on the decision making process rather than on the decision itself. This is deliberate. The school histories do not set out to identify "correct" solutions; at times the teachers' eventual decision is omitted altogether, and there is seldom any detailed follow-up. The reason is simply that both the decision and its long-term results are determined by a multitude of factors peculiar to each individual school. Describing a success story in the school history would not mean that the same solution would be appropriate in the

8

reader's school. Hence, the aims are: (i) to identify controversial issues in the education of children whose behaviour or educational progress gives cause for concern; (ii) to describe some of the ways in which teachers can look critically at the effects of the provision they make for these children; (iii) to discuss how aspects of a school's own organisation can create problems for the children they are designed to help; (iv) to describe some of the personal and personality factors which facilitate or impede innovation; (v) to open up discussion about the most appropriate use of external support services.

The case histories of children describe a range of problems. In many instances the child history develops the main theme of the previous school history, showing the effect of particular policies or decisions on an individual. The central aim is to direct attention to the school's potential contribution in meeting the child's needs, even when the present problem seems to arise directly from massive disturbance or neglect in the family.

Again, there is no attempt to round off each history with a neat solution. In some histories questions are left unanswered and problems unsolved. To do otherwise would be unrealistic. The reality of problems facing teachers is that they must often make decisions on the basis of inadequate information. Even when all the information required is readily available, well formulated plans often fail to produce tidy solutions. Moreover, outcomes are of little relevance in the child histories, as in the school histories, if it is accepted that success or failure depends on the people who operate the treatment programme at least as much as on the programme itself. The histories are not, on the whole, about teaching methods and techniques, but rather about the underlying processes which determine the climate in which particular methods or techniques are applied.

Using the case histories Each case history is preceded by two or three main themes which identify the major issues arising from the history. At the end there is a list of ten to fifteen questions. These have five principal aims:

(*i*) to draw attention to some purely factual matters raised in the histories, for example questions relating to the law as it applies to children;

(*ii*) to draw attention to decisions based on incomplete information;

(*iii*) by highlighting problems in other schools, to alert teachers to the possible limitations of the facilities in their own;

(*iv*) to identify different ways of using the support services;

(*v*) to increase the teacher's self-critical understanding of his own motivation, and his sensitivity to the needs of children who fail to fit into the existing system.

The questions are intended for guidance only, and should be used with discretion. There is most certainly no intention that each one should be answered, nor that there can be any correct answer to many of them. The student or teacher reading the book on his own may find that the questions identify gaps in his knowledge, or that, together with the references given in some of the histories, they stimulate him to further reading. The lecturer using the histories in a seminar group will select questions for more detailed discussion from what he knows about the previous experience, skills and interests of the members. The questions selected for further discussion in a group of students who have just completed their first teaching practice will be quite different from those selected for experienced teachers taking an M.Ed. degree. The most appropriate questions for an advanced course on personal counselling will be different again.

Conclusions

This book is about children whose educational failure or disturbing behaviour challenges their teachers. It is also about teachers who have the energy — and the personal courage — to question the system they are currently operating and to modify it in the light of their answers. It would be unrealistic only to describe good practice and successful innovation, but the underlying current is, I hope, optimistic. The contribution of teachers in separate special schools is not under-rated by an insistence that special education is an activity which takes place in many ordinary schools as well. In its literal sense, special education is neither more nor less than good education, and good education is neither more nor less than education which is appropriate to the needs of the individual. This book aims to show some of the ways in which teachers can modify their own ideas and draw up programmes to provide more appropriate educational experiences for their most difficult pupils. My hope is that this will give others the confidence to do likewise.

David Galloway
September 1979

References

Boyson, R. (1974) The need for realism, in Turner, (ed.) *Truancy*, Ward Lock Educational: London.

Bugler, J. (1976) Janet and John for the high jump, *The Guardian*, 30 January.

Cashdan, A. and Pumfrey, P. D. (1969) Some effects of the remedial teaching of reading, *Educ. Res.*, **11**, 138–42

Department of Education and Science (1977) *Statistics of Education*, 1976, Vol. 1, *Schools*, HMSO: London.

Department of Education and Science (1978) *Special Educational Needs* (The Warnock Report), HMSO: London.

Galloway, D. M. (1976) Size of school, socio-economic hardship, suspension rates and persistent unjustified absence from school, *Brit. J. Educ. Psych.*, **46**, 40–7.

Galloway, D. M. and Goodwin, C. (1979) *Educating Slow-Learning and Maladjusted Children: Integration or Segregation?*, Longman: London.

Gillham, W. (ed.) (1978) *Reconstructing Educational Psychology*, Croom-Helm: London.

Hargreaves, D. (1967) *Social Relationships in a Secondary School*, Routledge and Kegan Paul: London.

Hargreaves, D., Hestor, S. K. and Mellor, F. J. (1975) *Deviance in Classrooms*, Routledge and Kegan Paul: London.

Osterling, O. (1967) *The Efficacy of Special Education*, Scandinavian Univ. Books, Uppsala.

Reynolds, D. and Murgatroyd, S. (1977) The sociology of schooling and the absent pupil: the school as a factor in the generation of truancy, in H. C. M. Carroll (ed.) *Absenteeism in South Wales: studies of pupils, their homes and their secondary schools*, University College, Faculty of Education: Swansea.

Rose, G. and Marshall, T. F. (1974) *Counselling and School Social Work*, Wiley: Chichester.

Rutter, M., Cox, A., Tupling, C., Berger, M. and Yule, W. (1975) Attainment and adjustment in two geographical areas: I The prevalence of psychiatric disorder, *Brit. J. Psychiat.* **126**, 493–509.

Sampson, O. C. (1975) *Remedial Education*, Routledge and Kegan Paul: London.

Spooner, R. (1979) Pastoral care and the myth of never-ending toil, *Education*, 2 March, 251–2.

PART II
Primary schools and their pupils

White Horse Infants School

Main themes

1 The idea of "parents as partners" may be accepted in theory by teachers; except in "good" areas, however, it is unlikely to be accepted by parents without a great deal of imaginative effort from the school.

2 Adequate home–school liaison is difficult if the teachers rely entirely on outside agencies for information about the home.

Beatrice Richmond, head of White Horse Infants School had always prided herself on her school's welcoming attitude to parents. On taking over the headship ten years earlier, one of her first actions had been to pull down the wall-notice saying "No parents beyond this point" which had always blocked parental access beyond the entrance lobby. To be fair, the notice had never blocked access to the middle-class and more articulate parents; they had always ignored it, going straight to their children's class teacher or the head as they preferred. The parents who had been intimidated by the notice were the working-class parents whose co-operation the school most needed to enlist.

There had, of course, been progress since then, yet Mrs Richmond had to acknowledge, as she reviewed the last two years' work that it had not developed as she had hoped. As a life-long supporter of the Labour Party's left wing she had always believed in the power of education in reducing inequality. One of the ways she saw this happening was by the school co-operating with parents in helping their children to overcome the disadvantages they themselves had suffered as children. It followed that the greater the contrast between the school and the homes of its most disadvantaged pupils, the greater the reduction in the gap between the attainments and aspirations of children at the two extremes in her catchment area.

That at least was the basis for her hopeful idealism when she was appointed at the rather young age of 35. Now, ten years later, she saw minor reductions in poverty amongst families in the school's catchment area, but no reduction in the gap between privileged and under-privileged. Both in educational attainment and in general standards of health and behaviour the children from owner-

13

occupied houses remained as far ahead of those from the high-rise flats and the estate of semi-detached council houses as ever.

Admittedly standards at the school had improved noticeably over the last decade, she thought, as she leafed through the annual reports on the reading ages of children leaving for the junior school. Yet this did not obscure the fact that the range of attainments remained unaltered, nor that you could still make a good guess about whether a child's reading age would be in the top or bottom half of his year group if you knew his address. It reminded her of a research report she had read recently about the effects of secondary schools on their pupils. Successful schools could raise overall standards, the report claimed, while unsuccessful schools had the reverse effect, yet neither reduced the gap between the most able and the least able pupils.

Although Mrs Richmond no longer felt the same confidence that school could do anything to overcome the social and aspirational divisions in society, she still felt that school could and should make further efforts to compensate for the more obvious examples of deprivation and disadvantage. Discussing it with Julia Storey, the teacher who had completely re-organised the school's approach to language development and the teaching of reading following publication of the Bullock Report, she tried to analyse the issues.

There had always been the perennial difficulty of attracting into school the parents whose children gave them most cause for concern. These parents were generally the least likely to come in the first place. Much of the problem, though, was that they had never been very sure of the reasons for inviting the parents. Apart from the fact that school—home co-operation was A Good Thing, Beatrice Richmond suspected that many parents went away from open evenings no wiser about their children's progress or difficulties than they had come. At best, meetings with teachers served to make these parents feel that the school had their children's interests at heart; at worst, however sensitively and tactfully the teachers tried to broach the subject, they felt that the school was using their visit to complain about their child's behaviour or lack of progress.

"We've got to think more clearly why we want to see parents", Julia said. "First we want parents to feel a pride in the school, to regard it as part of the local community. Second, we like to think we may have something useful to offer parents that will help them improve the child's educational experiences at home. Third, we want help from parents, in alerting us to things at home which might have an unsettling effect on the child at school."

The head agreed. She thought they had in fact been quite successful in meeting the first of Julia's aims. Relations with the local community were good; the annual fund-raising fete was well supported; on the infrequent occasions when local shopkeepers or householders rang up to complain of a child's bad behaviour, it was without rancour on either side. Mrs Richmond thought they were partially successful with Julia's third aim. Parents generally told them when something serious happened, like family break-up, death or serious illness, but they not infrequently found that parents overlooked some less obvious sources of stress. One recent example was the six-year-old boy who stopped making an effort to read when he found that his four-year-old sister was overtaking him at home. The teacher only realised this a year later when the sister started school, and overheard her class teacher saying how bright she was.

They seemed to have made no progress, however, with Julia's second aim. A lot of parents probably had a vague feeling that teachers would be willing to help them with advice if necessary yet this vague feeling was only converted into requests for advice when the family faced some sort of crisis. Home and school were still two quite separate worlds. The idea of parents as partners, advocated so eagerly by the Warnock Report was an admirable theory but much harder to convert into practice. One thing seemed clear to the two teachers. The gap would not be bridged by further invitations to parents to come to the school. If the mountains would not go to Mohammed, then Mohammed must go to the mountains.

Home visiting had not been a particularly controversial issue at White Horse Infants School, as at some other schools. On the whole it was left to the education welfare officer (e.w.o.) who acted as go-between when parents did not come into the school on their own initiative or failed to answer inquiries from the school. Mrs Richmond's recent conversation with Julia Storey, however, made her review this policy. If the school was going to have any influence on parents, she argued, it would have to start early. There seemed no better time than the term before a child started full-time attendance.

The child's impending start would give a teacher an excuse to visit, ostensibly in order to discuss with the mother how she could help to prepare him for school and to tell the teacher about any special needs. The visit would give the teacher a chance to identify children under stress from emotional disturbance or social deprivation, and their mothers could then be encouraged to join the school's toy library. Follow-up visits would be made to these families to help them recognise how their children could benefit from different toys as they grew older, and how they themselves could encourage their children's language development by talking and playing.

"The theory's all right", Julia said as the head developed her ideas, "except that a lot of the families we're talking about don't have time to talk to their children, let alone play with them. But where on earth do we find a teacher to carry out this school−home liaison work you are proposing?" Mrs Richmond appeared to be looking at her hands as she replied carefully that Judith had kindly agreed to take a full-time class from next year. Judith was the school's deputy head who only taught half a timetable. The other half of her time was in theory spent on administrative duties and filling in for teachers on courses or off school because of illness. In practice, most of the staff thought she had an easy number, that her time could be used more effectively.

"So if Judith takes a class full-time", the head continued unperturbed by Julia's raised eyebrows, "that leaves someone else free in the afternoons as a home−school liaison teacher. How do you feel about the idea?"

Questions

1 It is said that middle-class parents ignored the notice saying "No parents beyond this point". Can you think of other instances where middle-class parents get information or advice from school that is not readily available to less articulate and less well informed working-class parents?

2 Can you think of ways your school discourages the parents whose co-operation it needs most? Have you, as a teacher, done anything to discourage these parents?

3 Is it realistic to hope schools might reduce inequality?

4 Would you expect it to follow that "the greater the contact between school and the homes of its most disadvantaged pupils, the greater the reduction in the gap between the attainments and aspirations of children at the two extremes in the catchment area"?

5 Is there confusion about the aims of inviting parents to school at your own school?

6 Do you agree with Julia Storey's reasons for wanting to see parents?

7 How do you assess the quality of a school's relationships with its local community? Are the ways implied here the only ways — or the best ones?

8 Do you agree that the gap between the school and the parents of disadvantaged pupils could not be bridged by further invitations to the parents to come to school?

9 Are you happy with the idea of a home—school liaison teacher, with a major responsibility for enlisting parents' co-operation before their children start school? What are the likely difficulties?

10 What do you infer about the school's chain of responsibility from the penultimate paragraph?

Vicki

Main themes
1 Severe difficulties at home do not necessarily result in similarly severe difficulties at school.
2 It is easy to overlook specific learning difficulties that have nothing to do with home circumstances if home circumstances provide an easy explanation for the child's lack of progress.

Julia Storey came away from the Lamberts' flat feeling anxious and bewildered. Physical conditions in the home had been adequate, though there was a general air of neglect. The two children looked healthy enough, and there was evidence of a recent meal with meat and two veg on the table. There were no toys and no evidence of Vicki or her three-year-old brother drawing or painting, but this was not too uncommon; it was one of the needs the toy library had been set up to meet. The children did not seem particularly subdued once Julia had been in the flat for five minutes.

The worrying thing had been the parents' physical and mental condition and their attitude to the children. Mrs Lambert was a tense, excitable lady who launched into a tirade against the local social services department within two minutes of Julia's arrival. It appeared that her doctor and the "welfare" people wanted her to go into a mental hospital, but she had naturally refused. She had her husband and children to look after, didn't she? From time to time she jumped up from her chair and ran almost hysterically out of the room shouting at the small boy who had wandered upstairs and was stamping on the bedroom floor. She had twice tried to do away with herself, she claimed, but both times " 'e" had stopped her.

" 'E" had listened impassively while his wife talked about her problems. When she listed her ailments over the last five years he caught Julia's eye and nodded wearily. They included double pneumonia, cancer of the stomach, a broken leg and a thyroid disorder. As if all that wasn't enough, Mrs Lambert continued remorselessly, her husband had been out of work for nineteen years with depression and now the hospital had diagnosed cancer of the liver. Again Mr Lambert nodded wearily.

Three-quarters of an hour after her arrival Julia Storey suddenly remembered, as Mrs Lambert paused for breath, why she had come. Mrs Lambert continued her account of her husband's last visit to the hospital unabated. Julia left half an hour later having failed completely to find out anything about Vicki. She had also failed to tell Mrs Lambert anything about the school, let alone interest her in the toy library.

On her return to school she telephoned the social services area responsible for the flats where the Lamberts lived. After a short delay she found herself talking to a senior social worker who had known of the family for three years. He confirmed that most of what Mrs Lambert had said about her own and her husband's health was true; Mr Lambert would probably not live more than a year, possibly only six months. Mrs Lambert, he thought, coped with life better than appeared to be the case at first sight. Neither of her attempts "to do away with herself" had come near success; on the first occasion she had waited until her husband's arrival home from hospital before trying to swallow a handful of sedatives, and on the second she had woken him up to tell him that she had done so. She then made a noisy attempt to stop him calling the ambulance which was clearly not intended to succeed.

The social worker acknowledged that the children were "at risk" but did not think active intervention was indicated at the moment. "It's very doubtful if we would have a case", he told Julia, "and even if we did I'm not sure that I would want to take action unless things deteriorated quite a long way. We've got to balance the sort of care we would be able to offer them with the fact that against all the odds they do seem to be developing fairly well at the moment."

Julia made one more visit to the Lamberts' before Vicki started school. She found Mr Lambert deteriorating and his wife as tense and excited as ever. Vicki seemed less forthcoming than on her first visit, but nodded obediently when Julia asked if she was looking forward to starting at White Horse School.

When she did start school, Vicki appeared to settle in well. She was rather unsure of herself for the first few days, but this was not altogether surprising in view of the fact that she lived on the sixth storey of a high-rise flat and had never attended a nursery school or play-group. She seemed to mix easily with the other children and joined in the usual range of classroom activities. Her language was rather immature, she sometimes seemed not to hear what was said to her, and she seldom took any active part in the language work her teacher did with the class. The school doctor carried out the usual hearing test with which she screened all pupils, and as this indicated no problems, her teacher attributed the apparent mild unevennesses in her development to her family circumstances.

Towards the end of her first full year after the reception class, Vicki's second year teacher was less happy about her progress. Socially she remained a co-operative girl, well integrated with the rest of her class. She had had a set-back after Christmas when her father died, but she seemed to get over this after a few days of tearfulness. The thing that was worrying her class teacher was her lack of progress in reading. She could write tidily and quickly and her number work was nearly average for her class, but she still seemed an almost total non-reader. Julia Storey and Mrs Richmond, the head, thought that if this was Vicki's only problem both Vicki herself and the school had a great deal for which to be thankful.

Towards the end of her final year at the school Vicki's reading had still not improved, and her third class teacher, Marion Knight, was getting seriously worried. "Of course it may be that she's simply not very bright", Mrs Richmond remarked as they were discussing her lack of progress in the staff room. "That would explain why she seems to have been so unaffected by such dreadful conditions at home; I understand from one of the dinner ladies that her mother's getting worse." Marion Knight was not convinced. Dull children usually had problems with number work as well as reading; dull children seldom took as active a part in social activities as Vicki.

The following week she happened to overhear Vicki and another girl reading together. "Br−i−ng", said the other girl helpfully; Vicki looked at her blankly. "Br−i−ng", said the other girl more quickly, drawing the sounds closer together. Still Vicki failed to get the message. "Bring", said the other girl at last. Vicki's face lit up. At playtime the teacher asked Vicki to stay behind and read out a list of words broken down into sounds, asking Vicki what each one was. Vicki was able to recognise some of the three letter words, but got the vowel sound wrong with nearly half of them. Anything more complicated was completely beyond her unless she had a contextual clue, for example when the teacher looked at the w−ind−ow as she spelt the word out.

Next Marion Knight asked Vicki to tell her the sound that each word began with. She started with nonsense words: "vopple" she said. Vicki looked puzzled and asked, "W?" in a hesitating voice. Even when the teacher started saying familiar words such as "pot", "lorry", "dog" Vicki had great difficulty in identifying the initial sound. Marion was thoroughly puzzled and tried the same tests on the other two children whose reading was as bad as Vicki's. Both were boys who Marion privately thought were much less bright than Vicki, but neither had the slightest difficulty with either task.

Vicki's teacher took the problem to the head. "I can't help wondering", she said, "if we haven't all been so worried about Vicki's home circumstances that we have overlooked the real reason for her backwardness in reading. She doesn't seem to be able to put sounds together at all, and she's just as bad at discriminating between sounds." Mrs Richmond listened with growing interest. Marion thought that games like "I Spy" would help Vicki learn to recognise the different sounds in words, but she wanted specialised advice about what other materials would be likely to help. Was there, she asked, an advisory teacher who might be able to give her any more ideas?

The head looked doubtful. It was only a month before the end of term and next September Vicki would be in the junior school. It might be better to leave contact with the advisory services to her new teachers. Meanwhile there was something else they could do before the end of the term, Mrs Richmond told Marion Knight, as she wrote a note to the school doctor asking for Vicki to have a thorough hearing check-up and explaining her class teacher's suspicions.

Questions

1 What are the aims of toy libraries? In what circumstances are they most likely to be successful?

2 Can you think of any other action which Julia Storey might have taken following her first visit to Vicki's parents?

3 Describe different and contrasting ways in which you think children might react to life in the Lambert family.

4 Are there any ethical problems involved, either in Julia Storey telephoning the social worker or in him providing her with as much information?

5 Can you think of examples of children whose attempts to do something aggressive or destructive seem always to be made at times when they could not succeed? Is there a parallel with Mrs Lambert's behaviour?

6 Do you agree with the social worker's view that it would be wrong to take Vicki into care, even if he thought he had a legally watertight case to present to the Juvenile Court?

7 How might Vicki's performance at school reasonably be attributed to her family circumstances?

8 What is the screening test which school doctors carry out? How can it miss some children with less obvious hearing difficulties?

9 What inquiries would you carry out yourself or request others to carry out on a child who is an almost total non-reader at the end of her second year at school? Can this sort of retardation be attributed to background factors alone?

10 Comment on the informal tests Marion Knight carried out on Vicki's reading. Can you think of children with similar difficulties which you or colleagues have failed to notice?

11 Would a test have identified Vicki's difficulty in auditory integration and auditory discrimination?

12 What possibilities would you wish the school health service to explore about Vicki's hearing?

13 What are the implications for future remedial work with Vicki? What methods would you use?

Elden County Junior School

Main themes

1 Economic restrictions can lead a school to look more critically and more imaginatively at its existing use of resources.

2 Remedial reading can be tackled in a number of quite different ways.

The assistant education officer (a.e.o.) at the other end of the telephone winced. "Don't you think it's a bit stupid", Pearl Ashley asked him with her customary directness, "you people at the office sending us a letter one day commending the Warnock Report and its ideas about most handicapped children always remaining in ordinary schools, and the next day another letter saying that you're sacking our part-time remedial teacher to save yourselves a bit of money?"

The a.e.o. had to admit to himself that the timing had been less than fortunate, but he was not going to admit that to Pearl. The Warnock Report, he defended himself, was merely pointing out what everyone already knew, namely that special schools could cater for no more than a small minority of children with the most severe special educational needs. There was no intention of closing any special schools down. And as Pearl must know, the cuts had been imposed by the new Tory government and there had been a full discussion with the teachers' unions about how they should be made. This was a slightly unfair jibe, as the a.e.o. was an active member of the Labour party and happened to know that Pearl was active in her local Conservative Association.

The conversation was predictably fruitless and Pearl found herself discussing with her staff how to cope with the loss of a valued part-time remedial teacher. The lady in question had left full-time teaching at Elden Junior School to have a family, but had jumped at Pearl's invitation to apply for a part-time vacancy some four years earlier. Unfortunately the authority had insisted on appointing her on a year to year contract as her post was, strictly speaking, above the school's establishment. As a class teacher she had been highly successful with some of the school's more difficult pupils and as a remedial teacher she not only made remarkable progress with almost all of the most backward children, but

21

also gave their regular teachers a great deal of practical help and advice.

"The question is whether we simply drop all our remedial classes, or re-organise ourselves to carry on making some sort of provision", Pearl told her staff. The staff were as disappointed as their head teacher. Claire Crawley, an energetic middle-aged lady who taught a fourth year class, said that if they dropped all remedial classes the number of children referred to special schools would go up by leaps and bounds. "I can think of three already who will need to go if we don't give them special help ourselves. Surely that will show them at the office that it's false economy to cut our staffing like this."

Pearl was more of a realist. She thought the immediate effect would be to prolong the waiting list for special schools, with the long-term effect of encouraging empire-builders in the office and on the education committee who would see greater public popularity in new buildings, especially new special school buildings, than in part-time remedial teachers for ordinary schools. She agreed with Claire Crawley, though, that if they didn't do anything themselves they would have to refer more children for special school education.

What she did not add aloud was her private view that this would have a bad effect on staff morale. All the nine teachers on her staff took pride in their work and a child's removal to a special school was always accompanied by a sense of disappointment and failure. Fortunately, the educational psychologist realised this and spent a lot of time discussing the different possibilities with Pearl, the class teacher and the child's parents before they made a joint decision on what would be best.

Elden Junior School had an annual intake of between 50 and 70 children. So far they had managed to keep maximum class size to 30, with the majority slightly below. In the second year, though, the intake had been exceptionally low, and there were only 23 children in each of the two classes. Pearl herself had always made a point of taking every class for at least one lesson a week, as much to keep her own hand in as to give the class teacher a free period. There was also some flexibility when two year groups combined for PE. One of the nine teachers had a tenured part-time post, and her class was shared with the school's deputy head.

The deputy volunteered to take a class full-time, thus relieving the part-time teacher for remedial work on much the same basis that had always operated. The proposal was attractive administratively, but Pearl did not like it for two reasons. First, she knew that if the deputy taught full-time she would almost certainly have to give up teaching herself, and secondly she doubted whether the permanent part-time teacher was suitable for work with children with special difficulties.

She raised a different possibility. How about setting up a class that would cater full-time for the twelve or fifteen most retarded children in J2, J3 and J4? This would mean a moderate increase in size for the other classes but that would probably not make too much difference. "By the end of the first year we will know who is going to need special help", she said, "so we can direct them into the remedial class." Yet this idea also had its drawbacks. To start with, no one was very keen to have a class of backward children with an age range of three years; moreover, a lot of the children were also difficult and several teachers pointed out that they would react on each other if put together all the time. Finally, the old remedial teacher had always insisted that you could only do effective remedial work in groups of five or six at the most. "Each child", she had emphasised, "needs his own special programme, so you have to work with each one individually."

Pearl Ashley did not feel she was getting much further and shelved the discussion until they had all had time for reflection.

Later the same week Claire Crawley and Mike Daniels asked to see her in the lunch hour. Was there any possibility, they asked, of Mrs Ashley relieving them for one 30 minute lesson a day to take groups of children with reading or maths problems? They had worked out that between them they could give each child two or three sessions a week in a group of five or six, assuming that about a dozen children in each year needed this sort of extra help. It wasn't as much as they had been receiving, the two teachers pointed out, but it would surely be better than nothing.

Pearl played for time. "At the moment", she said, "one of you takes a J2 class and the other a J4. Would you each select your groups from the whole age range?" They had thought about this. They proposed that they should each have groups of J1 and J2 children on two days a week, and J4 and J5 on the other two. "And how much additional preparation time are you going to need?" Pearl asked. "You know how much time Ethel spends preparing work for her groups, not to mention the time she spends with the children's class teachers to make sure there is continuity between their remedial work and their ordinary work." Claire and Mike had thought of this too, but were not going to be drawn. "How much time do you think we ought to have?" they asked blandly. "Well I dare say you could tear yourselves away from Assembly", Pearl said briskly, "you both looked bored out of your minds while I was giving the children my little talk about helpfulness this morning! Anyway, I'll think about your idea and let you know."

"Actually we haven't quite finished yet", Mike interrupted. He explained that he had recently been on an after-school course on reading problems at the Teachers' Centre, and had heard about a project which claimed that counselling was as effective as remedial reading in improving children's reading ages. Pearl looked sceptical. The argument, Mike went on, was that most children who are backward in reading really need someone who will take a personal interest in them, to help them build up their confidence in themselves. What he and Claire proposed was that the children who needed remedial help would be allocated at random to one or the other of them, and that Claire's group would be a counselling group while Mike would concentrate on formal remedial teaching. "I don't mean just sitting round a table talking", Claire interrupted, "but I would like to use the time for the children to do things they enjoy, painting, modelling, playing games and so on, and let them talk more freely than they can in the ordinary classroom about things that may be bothering them."

Pearl Ashley was surprised. Claire Crawley usually had her feet firmly on the ground. It was most unlike her to suggest anything as weird as remedial teaching by counselling! On the other hand, she had to admit that Ethel often said it wasn't her remedial teaching that helped the children make progress, but coming for a talk and a bit of confidence boosting.

"All right", she said at last, "I'll have a talk with Mrs D. (the deputy) and see what we can arrange. It may be possible to give you the time you want, but I'm not sure about this counselling idea. Let me see the book you were talking about, and we'll talk about it together again."

Questions

1 What did the Warnock Report actually say about the integration of handicapped children in ordinary schools?

2 How did the Warnock Report define special education?

3 Can you think of children who have transferred to a special school from schools in which you have taught? What extra resources would have been needed to give these children appropriate help in an ordinary school?

4 If existing remedial teaching facilities were withdrawn at your present school, do you accept that at least three children might need separate special education?

5 Is the head's cynical view about special school waiting lists borne out by the position in your own authority?

6 In your own experience is a child's transfer to a special school accompanied by a sense of disappointment and failure on the part of his previous teachers? Or just a sense of relief?

7 What are the arguments for and against a small class of twelve to fifteen of the most retarded children? What is the over-riding consideration in coming to a decision?

8 In your experience, do difficult children react on each other? Does this imply they would be better off integrated into ordinary classes throughout the school, on the principle of "divide and rule"?

9 The head said the two teachers looked "bored out of their minds" in Assembly. In your experience, does school Assembly – unintentionally – help children learn how to cope with boredom?

10 Can you think of children whose general adjustment and educational progress might improve from personal counselling? How might the improvement be effected?

11 How would you select the children you thought might benefit from this approach?

Jimmy

Main themes

1 Children are often under stress outside school which teachers know nothing about.
2 Behaviour which seems silly and irrational to a teacher may be entirely logical and sensible from the child's point of view.

3 Difficult behaviour does not just lie "in" the child. It results from an interaction between the child and the people with whom he comes into contact — including his teacher.

Jimmy Darwin was one of the four children who Claire Crawley simply could not like. There was nothing particularly objectionable about him, she realised, but he was a continual source of irritation to her. The trouble, she supposed, was that she could not put her finger on the reason.

Jimmy was a talkative ten-year-old, just starting his final year at Elden County Junior School. His reading had been poor throughout his school career, and he was one of the few children who had successfully — if that was the word — defied the skill and efforts of Ethel Budgeland, the remedial teacher sacked by the authority to save money. There was no question, though, of considering him for a special school. This had been mooted at one stage, on the basis of his score on Young's Non-Readers Intelligence Test. They were about to refer him to the educational psychologist when someone thought of looking at his answer sheet. The pattern was so odd, that Pearl Ashley called him to her office to ask him about it. "Well you see, Miss", he explained awkwardly, "I didn't hear very well when Miss explained what we had to do, so I sort of . . . well, I just did what I. . . ."

"You mean you just guessed, Jimmy", said Pearl grimly. "Well, I think we'd better do it all over again now hadn't we?" This time Jimmy's score was well below average, but no more so than that of half a dozen other children in his class. "I never did trust the results of these tests", Pearl muttered, "I can't think why a good teacher like Ethel bothered with them."

Jimmy's reading ability was indeed poor for his age. With a reading age of about eight he was the most retarded in his class. He never tried to conceal his difficulty, although he appeared embarrassed by it. Claire often found difficulty in telling whether his questions and interruptions — which were numerous

25

— were based on a genuine failure to grasp the point she was explaining or to read what she had written on the blackboard. She did not want to discourage any child from asking questions if he did not understand something, yet with Jimmy she could not help wondering whether his questions were not designed to gain attention as much as to seek clarification.

If so, they were certainly successful as the other children were getting heartily sick of Jimmy. Twice in the last fortnight teachers had needed to intervene because Jimmy was being "sorted out" in the playground, and almost every question he asked in the classroom attracted hostile comments: "Can't you shut him up, Miss?", "He never bothers to listen first time", "Wrap up, Darwin!", "Go and find yourself a Beagle", and so on. Claire detested bullying but she couldn't help sympathising with the other children. Unfortunately for her peace of mind, she felt guilty about disliking Jimmy and as a result felt obliged to intervene on his behalf.

Another thing about Jimmy was that he was a successful clown. Recently he had got hold of a Ladybird reader from the recesses of Claire's stock cupboard and she had returned to the classroom after taking a telephone call to find him regaling the rest of her class with a staccato, dalek-like rendering of the non-adventures of Peter and Jane. "I know the text lends itself to a take-off", she said later in the staff room, "and personally I would consign any reading scheme with that sort of jerk-jerk language and those silly synthetic characters to the boiler; but that doesn't excuse him drawing attention to his backwardness like that!"

Jimmy had been placed in one of Mike Daniels' remedial reading groups. He went three times a week with one other child from Claire's class and three from different classes. Claire and Mike had not allocated the remedial children at random, partly because they both had two children they thought would benefit from being in a group with a different teacher. Mike's attitude towards Jimmy was brusque and no-nonsense. "You've come here to work", he told him, "and we'll have no stupid questions, and no wasting time." Jimmy looked at him, wondering whether to take up the challenge, but decided against it.

He had not been any trouble to Mike, but nor had he made much progress in the last six months. He seldom did anything to annoy the other children in the group. He joined in spelling and word-building games when asked; he completed his work-cards adequately; yet he never really appeared to have his whole attention on the task in hand, and he never seemed to remember anything for more than a day or two. This had been well illustrated when Mike gave him one of the Ladybird "Read it Yourself" books. With help he quickly learnt the fifteen or so unfamiliar words, and read the book with enjoyment. A fortnight later, however, he had not only forgotten them all, but seemed surprised by Mike's disappointment at the fact. The head had arranged that once a term she would review the progress of every child in the remedial groups with Mike, Claire and the class teachers. These reviews took place after school on three consecutive afternoons. Generally speaking the results were encouraging. Claire had tested Mike's groups at the beginning of the year and again just before the review, and *vice versa*

The results showed that over three-quarters of the children in both groups had made over six months' progress in reading age, and nearly half had made over a year's progress. On average Mike's group had made three and a half months' more progress than Claire's. On the other hand, class teachers of several children in Claire's group reported that their behaviour had been much more settled lately, whereas few of Mike's group seemed to have changed much one way or the other.

Jimmy, however, was one of the small number of children who had not made any real progress. Mike felt that he was getting nowhere with him − a feeling that was borne out by the test results − and Claire was, if anything, more exasperated than she had been after her first term with him. "Which means we need more information about him", Pearl concluded. "There's nothing in his medical record, nor in the record from the infants school to give us any help, so we'd better meet his parents again."

Strictly, the head was incorrect in saying that they ought to meet Jimmy's parents again, since no one present had so far met them at all. His mother had twice come to the school open evening, but the last time was in his second year at the school and his teacher then had since left without making a note of the meeting. He attended regularly, and so far as was known no agencies outside the school had knowledge of the family.

The first invitation to the Darwins was aborted by a note from the mother explaining that she worked in the afternoons, so could Mrs Ashley manage one morning? The second attempt was successful, though Mrs Darwin came on her own as her husband could not have a day off work unless it was a real emergency. She admitted she realised Jimmy was not much good at reading, but hadn't liked to make trouble by getting in touch with the school herself. At home he was a bit of a handful, especially with his gran. "Do you mean he always gets his own way with his gran?" the head asked. "Oh no. It's not that at all", Mrs Darwin replied hastily. "You see, her mind's gone, and she has to live with us because there's nowhere else for her, but she doesn't really know where she is most of the time; in fact I sometimes think the only thing she does know is that she and Jimmy don't get on together!"

Mike asked Mrs Darwin if she thought Jimmy was frightened by his grandmother's condition. His mother seemed surprised by the question, but then said slowly, "Well no, it's more like, more as if he only does it − only annoys her − when I'm about − as if he wants to make *me* do something."

It was obvious from the interview that Mrs Darwin had her hands full already, and would not be able to give the school much practical support in their attempts to help Jimmy. Nevertheless, the interview had been helpful. It seemed to Claire that Jimmy made his presence felt at home by teasing his grandmother in much the same way as he made it felt at school by drawing attention to his backwardness, taking on the role of class clown, and generally provoking the other children.

What was more surprising, Claire felt, was that neither she nor any of the other teachers had been aware of the fact that Jimmy's senile grandmother lived with the family. Normally this sort of information would have been picked up by someone from another child, if not from the child himself. It seemed as though Jimmy might be something of an isolate outside school. She started to wonder whether she shouldn't have pressed for him to be included in one of her informal counselling groups rather than Mike's more structured remedial class.

Questions

1 Can you think of children for whom you have felt active personal dislike, even though not all your colleagues shared your feelings? What was it about *you* that made you feel this way?

2 Intelligence tests have been called a lazy teacher's alternative to careful and systematic observation. Do you agree?

3 If you *must* use group tests, can you guard against being misled by unreliable results?

4 Describe Jimmy's behaviour in Claire Crawley's class in terms of reinforcement principles.

5 Do you think the rest of the class was really "heartily sick" of Jimmy? Or did they like his disruptive behaviour as well?

6 How do you react to nicknames, or puns on children's own names, with your own class?

7 Have you ever found yourself defending a child you dislike because you feel guilty about disliking him? Do you think Jimmy sensed how Claire Crawley felt?

8 Do you think Jimmy was deliberately drawing attention to his backwardness when he read the Ladybird book aloud?

9 In view of what was learnt about Jimmy's background, is his lack of progress in Mike Daniels' remedial group surprising? *How* might stress at home interfere with learning at school?

10 Do you agree that Jimmy's behaviour at home sounds similar to his behaviour at school?

11 Draw up a behaviour modification programme for Claire Crawley to apply with Jimmy.

12 Do you think Jimmy would benefit from counselling, either from Claire or from another teacher?

13 Would there be anything inconsistent in Claire trying to help Jimmy through counselling and simultaneously, applying a behaviour modification programme with him?

Doris Henley Primary School

Main themes
1 Bad theory may lead to good practice.
2 Teaching remedial groups on a withdrawal basis deprives a teacher of the potential job satisfaction which comes from having a class of her own.

William Senior allowed himself a moment of satisfaction after the remedial education adviser's visit. Normally he was critical of the service, particularly as his own school's general adviser was a secondary science specialist. "I'm sure he's a very clever man, but I don't know what he's got to offer us", he had told the chairman of his managers. The chairman had suggested diplomatically that perhaps the authority's chief adviser thought the staff of Doris Henley School might have something to offer the science adviser.

Yet the relationship had proved more fruitful than the head had expected. The general adviser made clear that his role was to help staff with any problems of professional development, such as secondment on courses, rather than particular problems in the teaching of certain subjects, and generally to act as a link between the school and the office. A fortnight ago he had told the head that the authority's remedial adviser had been expressing an interest in Beryl Scholey's work, and would like to visit.

Beryl Scholey had not been appointed as a remedial specialist but had shown a particular aptitude in this work. For her first two years in the school she had taught a class of nine-year-olds, but for the last four had been taking withdrawal groups for extra reading. She had a small room at the end of a corridor which was fully equipped with tape recorders, reading machines, arithmetic apparatus and a wide range of reading books and other language material. Her work was well known locally, and no fewer than four head teachers of neighbouring schools had sent their staff round to see her materials in the last year.

Since she started remedial teaching Beryl had run four groups a day, coinciding with the natural playtime and lunchtime breaks. For the first two years she had taken children in groups of twelve, each group spending four sessions a week with her. Thus, she was able to see 60 children a week. In the last two years, though, she had cut the size of her groups to six, so that each group now came only twice a week, though she continued to see the same number of children throughout the week.

Her reason for this switch was simple enough. She felt that a group of twelve was not very different from a small class, and allowed little opportunity for individual work programmes. She felt she could achieve better results by working more intensively with each child.

The immediate problem here was that she found she needed far more time to prepare her sessions with the smaller groups. She could no longer prepare a session for the whole group, as each child was following his own individual programme drawn up on the basis of his results on the diagnostic subtests of Daniels and Diack's Standard Reading Tests or the Neale Analysis of Reading Ability. She had got over this problem relatively easily, though, by arranging with the head and the class teachers that children would go to their groups a quarter of an hour after the start of each session. This gave her just sufficient breathing space.

The results had been encouraging. About half the children selected for the groups made sufficient progress within a year for Beryl and their class teachers to decide they could safely stop coming. The other half were regarded as having long-term problems who would probably need help, or at least support, as long as they remained in the school. At first Beryl had thought this second group consisted simply of the duller children, who would always have to struggle to keep up with ordinary class work. This was certainly true of some, but well over half seemed relatively bright children who were doing well in maths. And if they were bright at maths thought Beryl, who had hated the subject, they couldn't be all that dull intellectually.

As the general adviser had anticipated, the authority's remedial adviser was impressed with Beryl's work. "I can't think how I haven't heard of it earlier", he told Mr Senior. "This must be one of the best examples of remedial teaching in the authority." He went on to express strong criticism of "remedial" classes which operated on a full-time basis. "They create more problems than they remedy", he maintained. "Too often they just act as a sink for children who no one else wants to teach and even when that is not the case, putting all the backward children together creates as many problems as it solves." "Besides", he concluded, "how can you distinguish between the child who is backward in general development and the child who has specific reading difficulties but achieves good results in other areas, like numeracy?"

It was something of a novel experience to William Senior to have an adviser waxing lyrical about the progressive teaching at Doris Henley Primary School, so he contented himself with complimentary remarks about Beryl's energy, hard work and concern for the children, hoping at the same time that the adviser was not setting him up to agree that Beryl should be encouraged to apply for a recently-advertised advisory teacher job.

William Senior felt a little bewildered, therefore, when the next day Beryl came to tell him that although she enjoyed her work with the school's most difficult and backward children, she missed having a class of her own and would like him to consider the possibility of her taking a class of fifteen to twenty of the most difficult and most backward pupils at the start of the next school year.

She listened patiently while the head told her everything the adviser had said to him. She already knew the arguments, however, and agreed with most of them in theory. Her request had two reasons. First, she reminded Mr Senior that he had told her, shortly after her appointment, that every teacher worth her salt would want a class of her own. "Really, you shouldn't throw my own words back at me after all this time – I don't know where they've been!" he groaned. Second, she had been discussing the children in her groups with their class teachers and it had become very clear that a quarter of them accounted for three-quarters of the educational and behavioural problems which the class teachers had to face each day. "The point is", she persisted, "that about two-thirds to three-quarters of the children I take would probably make the grade anyway, given the time, while the remainder won't make it at all unless they have more intensive help."

William Senior knew the arguments; privately he thought there was nothing to choose between the argument for withdrawal groups and the argument for a full-time remedial class. Both could be disastrous with the wrong teacher and both could be highly successful with the right one. Life wasn't as cut and dried and amenable to educational philosophising as the remedial adviser seemed to think.

On the other hand, he thought Beryl under-estimated her effect on the 60 to 70 per cent of children who, she claimed, would make the grade anyway. Their teachers might well be able to cope with them pretty well at the moment – thanks to Beryl – but without any support from the withdrawal group the picture might be quite different. He put this argument to her, and she accepted that it might be true of some children, but probably not all.

They were unable to pursue the subject any further then because the head was called away to see a parent. He was in fact glad of the diversion, because he needed to think out the implications of Beryl's request. Ten days later he asked her to see him again and put forward a compromise. She could have her class of fifteen of the pupils who were most disturbing from an educational and behavioural point of view. They would be drawn from the J3 and J4 year groups. On four afternoons a week, however, he would like her to continue taking withdrawal groups as at present from the rest of the school. The number of children involved would, of course, be drastically reduced, but he thought it essential to continue to provide some form of support to the children and – more important – their teachers, and Beryl was the only person with the necessary experience. She asked who would be taking her class in the four afternoons when she had withdrawal groups. Mr Senior replied that he wasn't sure yet, but would discuss the possibilities with Beryl when he and his deputy started detailed planning for next year.

Questions

1 What do you regard as the role of the school's general adviser? Have you ever met your school's general adviser?

2 How can an authority publicise outstanding examples of good practice? Do you think teachers know enough about what their colleagues in other schools are doing?

3 What are your views on taking children for remedial sessions in groups of twelve compared with groups of six, bearing in mind that the latter halves the available number of sessions?
4 In your experience are remedial teachers given the children who could most benefit from the help they can offer? If not, why are the wrong children referred?
5 Beryl Scholey got over the problem of needing more time to prepare her sessions with smaller groups by arranging that the children would come to her from their ordinary class a quarter of an hour after the start of each session. Would this be possible in your school?
6 Is teaching a remedial group of six any less demanding than a group of twelve — or even an ordinary class of 30?

7 The results of Beryl Scholey's remedial teaching were considered encouraging. From the evidence given, do you agree?
8 Do you agree that if a child can cope with maths he cannot be dull?
9 Do you agree that maths is often taught badly because the teachers themselves were taught the subject badly and consequently disliked it?
10 Do you accept the remedial adviser's criticism of full-time remedial groups?
11 Do you agree with the head's view that there is really nothing to choose between arguments for withdrawal groups and arguments for a full-time remedial class?
12 Do you think the head's compromise solution was a reasonable one?

Richard

Main themes

1 No cases are hopeless — at least not in the short term.

2 Spending time on a difficult child may be a nuisance and unfair to other children — but less of a nuisance, and less unfair than the time spent sorting out the problems that result from not spending time on him.

3 Some children often look for trouble, but this does not mean they are disappointed if adults prevent them from finding it.

"And as far as I can make out, there's absolutely nothing anyone can do about it", Mr Senior told the group of disapproving teachers in the staff room. Visits from the community liaison officer for the local police force were regular and welcome. He had a nice down-to-earth manner with the children, helped the school in road safety courses and arranged cycling proficiency tests. Plain clothes officers from the C.I.D. were another matter altogether. They had called because they had "received information" as they put it, that a pupil from Doris Henley was making a nuisance of himself, almost every day, in the town's covered market and in both branches of Woolworth's. Their problem, they admitted openly enough, was that they could not throw the book at the little so-and-so because he was under age. They had also been quite honest about the real reason for their exasperation, which was neither the delinquency, nor even their inability to prosecute, but the boy's cheeky, aggressive, insolent "you can't touch me or I'll put my parents on to your bosses" attitude. "If you know any half-legal way to frighten the little beggar, I'd dearly love you to share it" one of them had said.

William Senor had not needed to be told the child's name. The Tipping family was not so much a thorn in the school's flesh as a running sore, he admitted to the officers, and the youngest, Richard, seemed to be the worst — which meant he was exceeding a pretty high standard of dreadfulness. Truancy had started young with the older Tipping children, but Richard had regularly selected the market and the streets in preference to the classroom before his ninth birthday. The older ones, too, had embarked on a delinquent career at an early age, but at least they had had the decency to wait until their tenth birthday before doing anything worse than stealing the odd bar of chocolate from the corner shop or

33

staying out until the police picked them up on the streets at midnight. Richard already had a string of twenty indictable offences to his credit, mostly stealing from shops in town, and had so often been picked up late at night that some officers no longer needed to ask him where he lived.

The social services department knew the family well, both because of their involvement with the older children and with Richard. The education department had pressed them to take Richard into care, and had even taken action in the Juvenile Court on the grounds of his poor attendance. The social worker, though, had taken the view that placing Richard in a children's home would help neither the boy nor his family, and recommended the magistrates to make a Supervision Order – a recommendation they had been thankful to accept having been told earlier the same day that the department had no vacancies even for two older boys on whom they had just passed Care Orders.

The Supervision Order had made no difference to Richard's attendance and his delinquent escapades seemed, if anything, to be getting more frequent. Since social services were disinclined to act, the detective sergeant had told the head that the police might have to consider making a Place of Safety Order. This would involve Richard being placed in care for a short time pending further investigations and another appearance before the court. Such an order, however, was a drastic step which the police were reluctant to take when social services already had the case in hand – in theory.

When he did honour his school with his presence, Richard could be contained without too much difficulty in the classroom. In the playground he had to be watched closely. There were two problems. First, his entrepreneurial spirit led him to identify smaller children with sweets, or anything else that he valued for that matter, and the teachers had to be on the look-out for incipient protection rackets. Second, he knew unerringly which other boys he could persuade to truant with him. On three occasions the class teacher had been surprised and upset – but more upset than surprised – to find himself three children short at the start of the session after play.

The family was disorganised – "a certain lack of structure" the educational psychologist had said with masterly understatement. Richard's mother had been married twice before marrying her present husband. She shouted loudly but ineffectually at her children, who came and went as they pleased. All the same, there was a certain unity in the family; mother and children cared about each other, and faced with interference from authorities such as the police, social services or the education department they closed ranks. It was this unity that had led the social worker to oppose the education department's request for a Care Order on Richard. His support had led to the family trusting him more than any of the other well- or ill-meaning do-gooders who came to the door, though their growing trust did not mean that they kept their appointments to see him any more regularly.

Given a reading book Richard appeared a non-reader; yet faced with the letters of the alphabet in random order he was able to identify over half of them. "This one goes with cat", he told Beryl with a toothy grin, pointing at "c". "So does this one", pointing at "a".

Special education had been considered, but rejected on the grounds that the

34

only sort of special education of value would be a residential school, and the family would not accept the idea. "And so", the head told Beryl and his class teacher Elaine Muller, "he's going to stay with us until or unless the police make a Place of Safety Order. The first question I want to consider is how we can hold on to him without letting him influence other children, and the second is whether we can actually teach him anything useful."

Richard was already attending one of Beryl's groups twice a week. He enjoyed these sessions, and co-operated well as long as he was fully occupied. The same applied in the classroom, except that it was more difficult to keep him fully occupied. Having Richard in her class had made Elaine Muller realise that children were wasting too much time standing by her desk waiting for her to mark completed work or explain things they did not understand. The rest waited patiently. Richard did not. He had also made her realise that she tended to overlook certain children. Richard had identified these children, and was trying to fade into the background with them − which mattered only because she felt certain he was planning something subversive.

Everyone agreed that Richard needed close supervision; particularly in the lunch hour and at playtime. Providing this supervision would be a nuisance, but less of a nuisance than sorting out the problems that resulted from allowing him a free rein. They decided that he would spend his lunch hour in the head's office, and his playtimes in a classroom under Beryl's or Elaine's direct supervision. They also decided to vary the nature of this confinement. If he had truanted the previous day he would be sat at a desk facing the wall, and no one would talk to him or give him anything to do. The same would apply if he had been suspected of anti-social behaviour, such as attempting to truant, disrupting other children, refusing to work, and so on. If, on the other hand he had attended school the previous day and had worked satisfactorily that day, he would be allowed to choose his own activity from some of the games and craft apparatus in the room. Attendance for a week would be rewarded by allowing him to invite another child to stay in with him, and play a game together. "We're not likely to get that far, so we can think of the next stage when we get to it", Beryl said resignedly.

To their surprise, they did reach that stage. Elaine was a bit disconcerted when the child Richard wanted to invite was a ten-year-old from Beryl's class with a reputation second only to Richard's. She kept her bargain, though, and as the two boys played snakes and ladders she heard a conversation that interested her. Harry asked Richard if he would like to be in Mrs Scholey's class. "No, not really", said Richard. Harry asked why − it was great in that class with only fourteen other kids! "You're a lot of hard nuts aren't you", answered Richard, "I'd be getting done all the time!" Harry denied it was like that. Mrs Scholey never even hit them! But Richard was adamant − "It's better here; there aren't any real hard nuts − and anyway Miss won't let me talk to them − that's why I haven't got done at all this week!"

Unfortunately Richard's progress was interrupted. A store detective caught Richard stealing yet again just before the shop closed at five o'clock. The police took him home, but he climbed out of his bedroom window and was picked up at three o'clock in the morning on the outskirts of the town. This time the police demanded that he be taken to a children's home and issued a Place of Safety Order.

Questions

1 What is the legal position about members of the C.I.D. talking to teachers about a child? What is the legal position about the police interviewing children in school?

2 Have you taught children who have openly defied the police? Is it adequate to attribute all the blame to the parents? Do you think the police themselves should share any of it?

3 What is the significance of the older Tipping children waiting until their tenth birthday before getting into serious trouble?

4 What is an indictable offence?

5 The social worker opposed the education department's view that Richard should be taken into care. Have you come across a similar case yourself? What were the arguments from the social worker's point of view?

6 What is meant by a Supervision Order? What are the legal implications of such an order?

7 In what circumstances do you think a Supervision Order might help a child like Richard?

8 Have you come across incipient "protection rackets" in your own school? How did you (or would you) handle them?

9 Richard's teacher was surprised and upset — "but less surprised than upset" — to find himself three children short at the start of the session after play. Comments?

10 Do you accept the implicit view that family warmth and unity can co-exist with severe disorganisation and persistent delinquency?

11 Describe the programme for controlling Richard in terms of reinforcement principles.

12 Richard made his class teacher aware of certain short-comings in her interaction with the children. Have the slow or difficult children you have taught made you more self-critical of your own teaching methods, and hence a better teacher? Is this a valid argument against sending these children to separate special schools?

13 Describe alternative ways to control Richard's potentially disruptive effect in school.

14 Do you think Richard really preferred not to be in Beryl Scholey's class, with the school's most difficult and backward pupils? If so, was this only because Beryl Scholey's pupils were older?

Dean Valley Primary School

Main themes

1 Good informal relations with parents are necessary, but they do not make formal records unnecessary.

2 It often takes a crisis, such as a head teacher's prolonged absence to make teachers aware of significant weaknesses in their school's organisation.

If Pat Muscroft had taught her spaniel not to regard all cats as legitimate prey everything might have been all right. Normally the dog's noisy, enthusiastic pursuit did not matter too much, but on the evening of the second day of the September term she had put her foot in a rabbit hole as she turned to shout at him − and now she was on her back with a broken leg and an as yet undiagnosed spinal injury; her newly-appointed deputy, Miss Thurston, would be acting head on her third day in the school.

With some justification, Miss Muscroft prided herself on knowing the parents of all the children in the 180-pupil school in a small town in the north of England. Both she and the school were, after all, part of the community. She also prided herself on good communications with her staff. There were some things she got to hear from and about parents which she decided to keep to herself unless the child's behaviour or poor academic progress made a full discussion with his class teacher seem desirable. Anything important, though, would go straight to the class teacher. The only flaws in the system were that Pat Muscroft stored all her information in her head rather than in her filing cabinet, and that class teachers got all their information at second hand. They never met parents themselves except for rather formal discussions on open night twice a year.

The fact that Angela Ogley's future teacher was on a course the day her mother called at Dean Valley School to ask the head to accept her onto the register, was unfortunate. Normally Mrs Ogley would have been introduced to Gail Murray before leaving and could have told her daughter's future class teacher herself that she suffered from haemophilia.

The head's only concern about admitting Angela was that she did not need to be in a special school. This anxiety had been allayed when Mrs Ogley produced a letter from a hospital consultant stating that in his opinion Angela should not require special schooling provided her teachers were aware of her condition and alerted a doctor if they noticed bruising or bleeding. As Angela had previously been attending an ordinary school, before her family moved to the area, there had seemed no question about admitting her.

Before leaving school that day Pat Muscroft left Gail Murray a note asking that she see her about a new pupil called Angela Ogley who would be starting the following Monday. She did not write any further details on the note, preferring to tell Gail herself. When she heard of the head's accident, Gail warned the secretary that Angela would be arriving. This was why Mrs Ogley and Angela were welcomed by the secretary on Monday morning with the words: "Oh yes, Miss Muscroft told us you would be coming; Mrs Murray's expecting you, Gail, and she's arranged for another girl in your new class to show you around the school before you go in to Assembly. "Mrs Ogley left, happy that communications at Dean Valley School were so good and the teachers so welcoming.

That lunchtime Angela tripped on a book that someone had dropped on the stairs leading up from the assembly hall. She fell awkwardly, bruising her shoulder and elbow. It did not seem anything out of the ordinary and the teachers could not understand why she made such a fuss. "I've got to go home", Angela kept saying, "Mummy will take me to the doctor." "We've got a right little hypochondriac here", another teacher whispered to Gail Murray as she asked Gail to comfort her. Eventually Angela calmed down and afternoon school started smoothly enough. At playtime, however, another child brought Angela to Gail, to show her an ugly red swelling on her elbow and shoulder. Suddenly fearing that it might be something to worry about after all, Gail asked the new deputy head to telephone Mrs Ogley, who was not at home. By the end of school the swelling was worse, and Angela's horrified mother rushed her straight to hospital.

In the circumstances it was perhaps understandable that Mrs Ogley should have complained to the education department, alleging negligence in Angela's teachers. The deputy head had to submit to an inquisition first from the principal school medical officer, and then from a senior adviser. Both accepted that the incident had arisen from an unusual and unfortunate set of events, but both thought that communications between the staff at Dean Valley should be improved. The senior adviser had asked to see what records the school kept on each pupil. He had suspected that the only formal records were in Miss Muscroft's head, but this was not true. There was little on children's personal circumstances – these were indeed stored in the heads of Miss Muscroft and the class teachers. Educational progress, in contrast, was recorded scrupulously, with more detailed notes of each child's achievements than he had seen for a long time.

The Ogleys were pacified by a visit from the school's education welfare officer and apologetic letters from the deputy and from the Chief Education Officer. The latter was written and signed by the adviser. The adviser too was pacified by his visit to Dean Valley. He no longer thought there had been any serious neglect, and he was impressed by the thorough manner in which Miss

Muscroft and her colleagues recorded educational achievements. Nevertheless, the teachers themselves still felt uneasy about the school's welfare system.

The incident with Angela Ogley made them realise how totally they depended on the head for all information about a child's family. Until now no one had worried about this because there was little that Pat Muscroft did not know about the local community, and she was quick to point out to class teachers the different ways in which different children reacted to family adversity. Now she would almost certainly not be fit to return to the school for six months and they had to fill the gap.

Another point which the deputy believed most emphatically was that part of a teacher's professional development involved meeting parents, explaining their children's progress and difficulties to them, and seeking their advice about reasons for difficulties the teachers themselves were encountering with the children. In her previous school the head had encouraged parents to get in touch with their child's teacher at any time and this policy had proved of benefit to both sides. It was very different at Dean Valley where they found the head's door – and ears – were always open but access to all other teachers was strictly curtailed.

The problem was how to fill the information gap left by the head's accident, and at the same time develop closer, more informal links between parents and class teachers, in such a way that Miss Muscroft would not feel undermined or offended on her return.

The adviser encouraged the idea, but he too warned that Miss Muscroft might find any changes hard to assimilate. "Her strength and weakness is that she's a one-woman band as far as parents are concerned", he confided. On the other hand, he did think that she appreciated initiative, and if something came from her staff she would probably support it. "We could start", said the deputy, "with a monthly newsletter to parents with a message from Miss Muscroft on the front page. She'd like to think the school was keeping in touch."

The first newsletter did indeed contain a message from Miss Muscroft. Moreover the message expressed the hope that parents would feel free to talk to the deputy or class teachers about their children at any time, and added that the deputy would always be available to see parents at the end of afternoon school.

The next stage, the deputy told the other teachers at her next staff meeting, is to think about whether we need any sort of formal system for recording information about children that might be helpful in the future. "In particular I would like to talk about the sort of information on a child's family or his personal circumstances which should be passed on to the new teacher at the end of each year, and also the sort which should be passed on to the secondary school."

Questions

1 At your school, do teachers store confidential information in their heads or is there an adequate system for recording it? Is the system used?

2 Was there any reason why Mrs Ogley should not have negotiated Angela's admission directly with the head?

3 As well as sending Gail Murray a note, what further action should the head have taken before admitting a child suffering from haemophilia?

4 By implication, there is one critical failing in the school's organisation, which is not even mentioned. What is it?

5 Would you fault Gail Murray's and the secretary's welcome to Angela and her mother?

6 Do you think the teachers at the school were negligent in any way?

7 How does your school record educational achievements? Does it record achievements as conscientiously as problems?

8 Do you agree that meetings with parents should be regarded as part of a teacher's professional development?

9 Does your own school produce a monthly newsletter for parents? If not, do you think this could be useful? If so, is it useful? Could it be improved?

10 What formal procedures are in use at your own school for passing on information about family or personal circumstances when a child changes class?

Dawn

Main themes

1 It is not always helpful to try to protect children from stress.

2 Teachers can help parents in their relationships with their children.

3 Attacks of a chronic illness can be precipitated by several quite different things

Angela Ogley was not the only child with a medical history in Gail Murray's class. Dawn Kembal had suffered from asthma since the age of three and was constantly having time off school to see the doctor. She missed a certain amount of schooling, mainly because she took far longer than other children to get over minor ailments such as colds or winter 'flu. At her infant school she had been absent for a total of four and six weeks in the last two years.

Dawn was a reasonably bright, extremely conscientious little girl. Gail's private view after teaching Dawn for a month was that she was too conscientious. She had heard a lot about under-achievement at college, but Dawn was the first girl she suspected of over-achieving. It made a pleasant variation! Most of the time she was able to take part in PE, but some days her mother would send a note asking that she be excused because of her asthma.

In her first term at Dean Valley, Dawn had few attacks at school. Before she started Mrs Kembal had given the deputy head an inhaler which Dawn could use once or twice a day if necessary at four hourly intervals. In fact, Dawn seldom asked to go to the office for her "puffer". The school doctor had seen Dawn and Mrs Kembal in the infants, and a note in her record card said that her asthma was associated with bronchitic infections and allergy to pollen in the hay fever season.

After Christmas Dawn's asthma seemed to get worse. She started asking for her "puffer" at least once almost every day, and was seldom able to do PE. In addition, she occasionally seemed breathless in the classroom and would grip her pen or the seat of her chair as she caught her breath. Her class teacher put it down to a cold she had developed just before Christmas, but the effects were lasting a long time.

41

A small incident two weeks after the start of the Spring term gave Gail cause for thought. Her classroom looked out on to the street and children standing by the window could see passers by. Dawn and a boy were sticking a painting on the glass when the boy pointed to Dawn's mum walking past the window. Dawn appeared to take no notice but five minutes later she asked to go to the office for her "puffer".

Gail Murray would probably not have remembered this incident had not Mrs Kembal come into school the next week to see her about Dawn. She wanted to know how her daughter was getting on, but did not seem very relieved at being told she was making good progress from an educational point of view. Gail asked if Dawn was helpful at home. She really wanted to ask what Mrs Kembal was worried about, but thought this would be an intrusion. To Gail's surprise, Mrs Kembal said that Dawn could be a little terror at home. She would often work herself up into a terrible state. At first Gail thought Mrs Kembal was talking about her daughter's asthma, but it soon became clear that she was talking about her temper, though this usually triggered off an attack of asthma.

When Mrs Kembal had gone, Gail felt that she was a good deal further from understanding Dawn than she had been before the visit. She wondered vaguely if everything would have been made clear if Mrs Kembal's interview had been with the head, now slowly recovering in hospital. Her doubts were increased soon afterwards, when Dawn's asthma at school became worse. On one occasion it disconcerted the other children and alarmed Gail so much that she took Dawn to the office to ask the secretary to call her mother. "She won't be at home, Miss", Dawn had interrupted, "she goes to see my dad at lunchtime". In surprise Gail asked Dawn where her dad was. "In hospital, Miss, he's been there for a week now with his stomach."

Dawn spent the rest of the day in the office with the acting head, as the secretary went home at half past twelve. She told the deputy that her dad had been ill for some time, but had got taken badly the previous week and had gone into hospital for an operation — "and me mum's been that worried, what with him and me and my asthma", she added between wheezes. The acting head looked at her sympathetically and asked what she liked grown-ups to do when she had an attack. Did she like them to talk, or just leave her to get over it. "Oh, I don't mind, Miss", Dawn answered, adding, "Talking's nice really, but I don't like it when they start fussing and worrying; my mum does that a bit, and it's awful because I know she's trying to help — it's as bad as when the other kids ask a lot of silly questions." Later in the afternoon the acting head asked if Dawn had been to see her dad in hospital. The little girl's face clouded. "No, Miss, my mum says it would upset me seeing him in bed and I would get another attack of asthma." Would Dawn like to see her father, the teacher asked? "Oh yes — but I can't, so that's that."

"So really her asthma is psychological", Gail said later that afternoon when Dawn had gone home. The acting head disagreed. She thought that Dawn was naturally prone to asthma, and would get it with hay fever or bronchial infections. That did not mean she could not also get it when she was under stress. The trouble was that she and her mother were reacting on each other, with Dawn adding to her mother's worries and the mother's anxiety making Dawn worse.

The acting head had suggested one thing to Mrs Kembal which she hoped would not back-fire on her. Out of Dawn's hearing she had asked Mrs Kembal if it would be possible for Dawn to see her father. "I really think that she will be less worried and fretful if she sees him than if she stays at home worrying about him", she told the mother. Mrs Kembal had been surprised at the idea; she thought hospital visiting would be frightening for a delicate girl like Dawn. "Well think about it, anyway", she had been told, "you may find that Dawn is much more able to cope with what she can see for herself than with what she is worried she might see if she went."

Next day Dawn went straight up to her teacher. "Please, Miss, I saw my dad last night, he's not too bad, really, and we talked for five minutes!" She was obviously delighted and relieved. Later that day Gail reminded Dawn of what she had told Miss Thurston about what she liked grown-ups to do when she had an attack. Dawn nodded, so Gail asked if she had ever told her mum. Dawn thought, accurately enough, that it would be difficult to explain to her, but added that Gail or Miss Thurston might be able to.

When Mrs Kembal collected Dawn that day she made a point of seeing Miss Thurston to tell her of the success of Dawn's visit to the hospital. The acting head promptly sent for Gail, so that Mrs Kembal could hear how Dawn had greeted her teacher that morning. "Tell me", she said as an older girl went to find Mrs Murray, "has Dawn ever told you what she likes grown-ups to do when she gets an attack." Mrs Kembal was surprised − it was something they just hadn't discussed. "You see", Miss Thurston went on, "we have the feeling that she feels happiest if everyone treats it in a very matter of fact way, just accepting it as one of the ordinary little nuisances of life without getting upset or making any fuss − and I wondered if that was what you had found".

Mrs Kembal looked worried. "Oh dear", she said, "you know I do get terribly upset when Dawn has an attack, it's so frightening, and there are times when I get sick worrying about her. Do you think she senses it and gets worse?" Miss Thurston smiled. "Dawn's a bright little girl", she said carefully, "she's bound to realise it if you're worried − just as you are bound to worry; asthma can be a very frightening thing. But I do think it mightn't do any harm if you could treat it in a more matter of fact way, trying not to let you and Dawn worry each other so much."

Questions

1 Have you taught children who seemed to need an excessive time to get over minor ailments? What were the reasons?

2 Is there such a thing as "over-achievement?" How do you justify under-achievement if you don't accept the idea of over-achievement? How would you define over-achievement?

3 Do you think there was a likely connection between Dawn seeing her mother through the window and having an attack of asthma five minutes later?

4 Gail Murray thought it would be an intrusion to ask Mrs Kembal what was worrying her. How could she have encouraged Mrs Kembal to give this information without appearing to intrude?

5 Have you ever asked a pupil who suffers from asthma, a stammer, alopaecia etc how he likes adults to react? If not, can you give reasons?

6 The deputy head disagreed that Dawn's asthma was psychological. Do you?

7 In the deputy head's place, would you have felt confident enough to advise Mrs Kembal to let Dawn see her father? Do you think you would have agreed with her view that this was desirable?

8 Can you think of other children who have been protected from anxiety or embarrassment by well-meaning adults — parents or teachers?

9 Why do adults often try to shield children from unpleasant facts? Is it really for the children's sake?

10 Can you think of children and parents who interact so as to aggravate each other's anxieties? How can this cycle be broken?

11 Can you think of children and teachers who interact so as to aggravate each other's frustration and/or anxiety? How is this cycle maintained, and how can it be broken?

12 Do you think Miss Thurston's advice to Dawn's mother was realistic?

13 Are there any other sources of help for Dawn and her mother?

Coalbrook R. C. Junior and Infant School

Main themes
1 Within limits, children achieve what is expected of them; they live up – or down – to their teachers' expectations.

2 More important even than resources, the biggest single obstacle to change is the *status quo*.

Coalbrook Roman Catholic Junior and Infant School had an unprepossessing appearance externally and internally. Surrounded on all sides by damp terraced houses built at the end of the last century, it merged effortlessly into its surroundings in the depressed inner ring of a depressed town in the north west. Being a Church school had not prevented 85 per cent of its pupils coming from within half a mile of the school, nor had it given the intake any sort of social mix.

The authority had told Grant Holbrook at his interview that funds would be available to give the school a much needed face-lift, but there could be no question of any radical alterations like raising the floors to enable children to see out of the windows. The face-lift would be confined to a coat of paint and a partition to give the head an office of his own. The previous head had shared with the secretary.

The chairman of the managers was honest about the school at the interview. "I'm afraid it's a run-down school in a run-down area", he told the applicants at interview, "but there's a future here for anyone who wants a small school which isn't threatened by declining numbers." The reason for the last remark was not that the birth rate of the Catholic population had fallen less steeply in recent years than the Protestant majority, nor even that the immediate catchment area was unaffected by the local council's programme for demolishing substandard houses. In fact, this programme had probably saved the school, since the new estates were growing up on land that had been derelict for ten years, less than two miles away, and the school would serve these estates.

As Grant Holbrook took his first detailed look at his new school since his appointment, he reflected that things could hardly get much worse. He had taken up his appointment in the Summer term, hoping that this would give him

45

time to prepare some sort of plan for the start of the next school year. One of the more pressing decisions would be the organisation of the infants department.

With only 150 pupils the school could not even be called one form entry, yet the three infant teachers regarded themselves – and were regarded by the junior teachers – as a self-contained department. Grant did not think it feasible to make any attempt at blurring the boundary lines, at least at this stage. The head of the infants department was also his deputy. Miss Tomms had been at the school for 30 years and although she had wisely decided not to risk the indignity of rejection by applying for the headship, she made it quite clear to the new head that she knew all there was to know about Coalbrook School, its children and its parents.

One of the other two teachers in her department was also nearing retirement – though not fast enough, Grant thought to himself. The third was a probationer who was rapidly losing any flair and enthusiasm she might once have had.

Standards in the infants department were low; the children unfailingly lived down to their teachers' expectations. The occasional child who excelled was likely to find himself labelled precocious. The problem was not one of unkindness but rather of apathy and an excessive kindness based on sentiment. These poor children come from such terrible homes that we've got to be nice to them, seemed to be the prevailing attitude. The infant department reminded Grant of a loosely structured play-group. As a result the children were bored, became restless and badly behaved as bored children usually do, and thus confirmed their teachers' conviction that they were not yet ready for anything more formal.

In fairness, the annual intake did contain more than its fair share of problems. Less than a quarter of the children had been to play-groups or nursery schools and a disturbing number were on the area health authority's "at risk" register. They seemed to fall into three roughly equal groups: a group of noisy, aggressive children who were either rebelling against the lack of stimulus the school was offering them, or perhaps simply continuing in school the same pattern of behaviour which they produced at home; second, a group who seemed to accept the school for what it was, making the best of a bad job and causing no one any particular concern; and finally, a group of quiet, withdrawn children who seldom played, seldom spoke and generally seemed locked in their own little shells.

Grant Holbrook's previous school had worked closely with the education department's psychological service. They had always been reluctant on the infrequent occasions when the psychologist suggested special education, but had always supported the recommendation in the end. Yet the worst of the children who had gone to special schools from his own last school had less severe problems than at least twenty of the children at Coalbrook. "It looks as if I might as well choose whether to decide that they're all ESN(M), delicate or maladjusted and get you to send them to special schools, or decide that they're all normal and keep them here. I've certainly no idea how to select one or two per cent for special schools from this lot", he told the psychologist. The psychologist laughed. "There won't be any places until next Easter if that helps your decision", he said.

46

The infants department had always divided its 80 pupils more or less evenly between the three teachers. When placed with one teacher they stayed with that teacher until they went up to the junior school in the next door classroom. Grant was determined that Miss Tomms should consider the possibility of a more flexible arrangement, designed to cater specifically for the school's more obviously withdrawn and retarded children. The existing arrangement had nothing to commend it beyond making the minimum possible demands on the skills and energy of the three teachers.

He saw two possibilities. First, two of the classes could be increased in size to 32 children, leaving the third with sixteen of the most deprived and disturbed. Second, he could leave all three classes with 26 or 27 pupils but combine them into two groups for certain activities each day. This would leave one teacher to carry out more intensive work with a handful of children withdrawn from each class.

Neither idea was completely satisfactory, the first because of the danger of creating additional problems by the mere fact of placing all the most worrying children together in a single class, and the second because of the difficulty in choosing activities for which to combine the classes in order to release a teacher for withdrawal group work. More basically, Grant doubted the capacity of any of the three teachers for the sort of systematic, structured approach he had in mind. What he wanted was a three-pronged attack on the children's language development, perceptual skills and social behaviour, but he knew Miss Tomms well enough already to feel certain that terms such as these would elicit a defensive reaction that would make change even more difficult.

Instead he told her (truthfully) that the chairman of the managers, the local priest, had asked for a statement at the next managers' meeting on the personal problems experienced by children in the school. He obviously would not be passing any names on to the managers, but it would really be extremely helpful if she would let him have a list of all the children whom she felt concerned about, with a brief note of their particular difficulty or handicap.

The list, when it arrived, contained the names of 23 children, and a comprehensive range of problems. The next stage was more difficult. Grant told Miss Tomms that he had taken the liberty of showing the list to the school's adviser. This was true. He also told her how impressed the adviser had been by the whole exercise, and in particular by the detail in her observations. This was not true, but the adviser had concurred with the head's idea. "In fact", Grant Holbrook continued, "he would like to meet us all to discuss whether it may be possible for the authority to do anything to help these children. He dropped a hint that there may be some extra money for equipment if we can persuade him that we could use it effectively. If we're going to get any of it, though, we will have to think whether it's possible to reorganise the classes to let one of you spend a bit of time working with a small group."

Miss Tomms sucked her lips suspiciously. She didn't see the need for advisers, still less for new-fangled equipment. On the other hand, she didn't really feel entitled to oppose the head's idea to discuss the matter. The head's aim was to get Miss Tomms to come to his own conclusion for herself and think it was her own. If she could be persuaded to tell him and the adviser that a class of sixteen children with the most difficult problems in the department would be no more of a handful than a class of 32 or more without these children, he would be half way there. The next hurdle would be the decision about which teacher should take which class. The last, and highest hurdle, would be using the time with small groups or a smaller class effectively.

Questions

1 If you had £10,000 to spend on the buildings of a Victorian school such as Coalbrook Junior and Infant, how would you spend it?

2 Most children lived within half a mile of the school. The new estates were two miles away. How would this fact affect the school? What implications does this have for the teachers' policy and practice?

3 Do you think 150 is a viable number for an infant and junior school?

4 What are the problems that can result from a teacher staying at one school as long as 30 years? Is there any case for a legal maximum of ten years in one school?

5 Have you come across talented children who merge into the mediocrity of the majority in order to avoid being labelled precocious by you or your colleagues?

6 What is meant by "excessive kindness based on sentiment"? Have you come across this in schools in which you have taught?

7 Do you know children who are expected to behave badly, who consequently do behave badly, and therefore confirm their teacher's conviction that they are badly behaved?

8 The problem children at Coalbrook seemed to fall into three roughly equal groups. Does this fit in with your own experience?

9 What is the "at risk" register?

10 Does the intake of a school like Coalbrook have any implications for the l.e.a.'s policy on special education?

11 Do you accept the head teacher's assessment that he had two main possibilities in re-organising the infants department? Do you agree with his reservations about each?

12 Do you agree that "a three-pronged attack on the children's language development, perceptual skills and social behaviour" is what is needed in an area like Coalbrook's? What methods and materials would you use?

13 How would you have set about securing Miss Tomms' co-operation?

Josey

Main themes

1 Repeated absence from school because of illness can sometimes be a sign of serious relationship problems at home.

2 Schools have an important supporting role to play in the treatment of such problems.

The infants class teachers at Coalbrook felt sorry for Josey Morris. She was always ill. In her reception year she had missed several weeks with some mysterious bone infection in her arm. It had been investigated extensively at hospital, but nothing conclusive was ever discovered, nor did her arm look swollen or discoloured, although she and her mother both complained bitterly about it. In her second year it was her stomach. This was also investigated, just as inconclusively. Now, in her final year in the infants department it was her leg. She had fallen over in the playground at school and had tripped again on the way home. For the last three weeks she had been hobbling about between her bed and an armchair, and was now awaiting a further hospital appointment.

When she did attend school she complained of headaches, sore throats, stomachaches and pains in her chest. The school medical officer had examined her, found nothing abnormal and left further investigations to the hospital. Once or twice it had crossed the teachers' minds that she might be malingering but if so she put on an extraordinarily good act.

Josey was regarded as one of the brighter children in the infant classes, but because of her prolonged absences and poor health was placed in the newly created class of 15 children, taught by a young teacher in her second year in the profession. She seldom played with any of the other children, preferring to work at a table on her own. Her mother seemed co-operative but rather over-anxious about her daughter's health. "Has she been alright today?" she often asked as she collected Josey from school.

Josey would probably never have been referred to the school's visiting psychologist had the elderly school medical officer not been taken ill and replaced temporarily by a younger lady with different ideas. She saw Josey on her first visit to the school, not because she had an appointment, but because Josey was complaining of stomachache. Hearing the history from the head, Grant Holbrook, she wrote the psychologist a letter asking if this could be "the psychosomatic disguise in school refusal?" By this she meant that she wanted an opinion as to whether Josey's real or imagined ailments could be a way of avoiding school attendance and staying at home with her mother.

The psychologist and the head saw Mrs Morris together. She went through all her daughter's ailments and hospital investigations; she had to admit that nothing conclusive had so far been discovered. "But we're hoping they find what it is this time, with her leg", she added hastily. Josey was the youngest of three children and Mrs Morris readily admitted that she felt closer to her than to the older two, perhaps because of all the worry she had been since starting school. "You mean, all this only began when she started school?" Mr Holbrook asked in surprise. "Yes, funny isn't it?" answered Mrs Morris.

Another point to emerge as the interview progressed was that Josey hadn't been ill at all during the summer holiday, nor, come to think of it, in the previous Easter or Christmas holidays. That too, thought Mrs Morris was funny, but lucky really as it meant she could play out in the street with the other children. The psychologist asked what happened when Josey was ill at home. Did she spend all day in bed, or did she come downstairs and help mother? Mrs Morris was quite clear about this. Josey always tried to help — she would come downstairs if she possibly could; naturally Josey couldn't do too much, but she, mother, always spent as much time with her as possible. Mrs Morris' face lit up as she talked of the time she and Josey spent together when her daughter was ill. In contrast, there was distress and anxiety on her face as she told them how she worried whether Josey would be all right when she left her at school.

"You do realise, don't you, that Josey's education is suffering badly from missing so much school", the psychologist said. "I'm afraid that if we can't do anything to help her feel fit enough to come more regularly, the authority may start thinking whether a residential school for delicate children would be a good idea." Mrs Morris was not a bit enthusiastic about that idea.

"Well we've got to recognise that there is a problem, and see what we can do about it", the psychologist continued. "To start with, Josey has been having investigations at hospital on and off for the last two years, and it seems from what you say that they haven't discovered anything. Now I'm not saying that Josey has been putting it on, but I do think she enjoys being at home with you more than being at school, and I think some of her illnesses may have been connected with this." Mrs Morris nodded doubtfully.

"It seems to me", the psychologist continued, "that you can find out for yourself quite easily whether Josey really is physically ill or whether her illness is caused by wanting to stay at home with you. Whenever she says she's not well enough to go to school, don't argue with her, but tell her that if she's not well enough to be at school she must stay in bed all day. Take her meals up to her and give her drinks when she wants them, but *don't stay with her* between nine o'clock and four o'clock — the time she should be in school. If she really is ill she'll be glad to stay in bed, but if she's not she will quickly get bored and ask to get up and go to school. When she is at school I'm going to ask the teachers to do

50

the same sort of thing. If she complains of being ill she must lie on the couch in the medical room, but she mustn't have anything to read, nor must she have children or teachers coming in to talk to her. If she's ill she'll want the rest, but if she's not she will get bored and ask to join the other children again."

It was fairly obvious both that Mrs Morris saw the logic in what the psychologist was suggesting and that she was going to find it extremely difficult to carry out. The psychologist offered to ask a social worker from the child guidance clinic to see her regularly for the next few weeks, but she declined. "No thank you, love", she replied, "if Josey's going to get better I've got to help her myself." She did ask, though, that the psychologist should write to the hospital consultant to explain what he had suggested and to ask him to say whether any of the tests they were carrying out next week were positive.

The psychologist's letter to the consultant paediatrician was diplomatic. "Naturally", it ran, "I explained that the medical diagnosis of the pain in this little girl's leg was entirely your responsibility. Nevertheless, if Mrs Morris is correct in saying that the results of all previous tests have been negative, it does seem possible that there may be a psychosomatic element, especially as all the trouble seems to have started since she began school and she is apparently healthy during the holidays." The letter concluded by explaining the advice that had been given to Mrs Morris and looked forward to receiving the consultant's valued advice.

His reply came the following week. "As you surmise", it ran, "we have carried out numerous tests in the last two years, and all have been negative. Your letter saved us from doing any more. Preliminary investigation reveals no organic basis to the pain in her leg and I do not think any further investigation necessary. Mrs Morris seemed most relieved that you were advising her. We ought perhaps to have referred her to a psychiatrist ourselves two years ago, but I am happy to leave the case with you." Copies had gone to the G.P. and to the school medical officer.

Josey had spent one day in bed and then stumped grumpily off to school with no trace of a limp. At school she complained of a headache, but asked to rejoin her class after one hour in the medical room. At the first follow-up interview her mother was delighted. It was the first time since her daughter started school that she hadn't been worried sick about whether she was fit to go.

At the second follow-up a month later she was happy that Josey was still free of physical symptoms but concerned that she was starting to be defiant and obstinate at home. Her teacher had noticed a similar development at school. Josey was no longer a quiet, pathetic little thing who was always ill. She was coming out of her shell, talking too much and too noisily, interfering with other children's work, being rude to the teacher, in fact being a thorough nuisance. "I'm not sure I didn't prefer her as she was", her teacher told the head and the psychologist just before Mrs Morris arrived.

Questions

1 Have you taught children who have had repeated investigations at hospital — always with no result? Did you ever suspect a psychosomatic basis?

2 Is it ever correct to say that children with psychosomatic illness are malingering? What is the difference?

3 Describe the different ways in which a mother's anxiety about her child may affect the child's behaviour – and hence increase the mother's anxiety. How can this sort of cycle be broken?

4 Are there any children in your present class whose colds or other ailments could be a mild version of what the school doctor calls "the psychosomatic disguise in school refusal"?

5 The psychologist and the head saw Mrs Morris together. What are the arguments for and against a joint interview of this sort?

6 Josey was the child to whom her mother felt closest. Have you come across "problem" children who seemed to have a closer, more intense relationship with a parent than their siblings?

7 Mrs Morris appeared remarkably lacking in insight at her first interview with the head and the psychologist. Explain some of the ways in which people protect themselves from unpleasant or painful ideas or feelings.

8 Do you think it was improper of the psychologist to have mentioned the possibility of a residential special school at the first interview?

9 Do you think the psychologist's advice to Mrs Morris and the head was logical, or practical?

10 The paediatrician said Mrs Morris seemed "most relieved" that the psychologist was advising her. Why do you think she was so relieved?

11 Why do you think Josey's behaviour might have changed in the month between the second two follow-ups? What advice might be given to the teachers and to Mrs Morris now?

Croft House Primary School

Main themes

1 If the l.e.a.'s support services are to provide a useful service, class teachers must have direct access to them.

2 Effective use of support services also requires careful co-ordination and discussion within the school.

3 Meetings can create the problems they are designed to solve.

Joe Gardiner had always placed a high priority on establishing good relationships with the authority's advisory and support services. His eagerness to co-operate with them was reciprocated; Croft House Primary School enjoyed a good reputation in the authority. Placing a high priority on co-operation with the support services implied to the head that he should act as link with them himself.

The service he saw most of was naturally the education welfare service whose officer called at least once a week, and often more, to hear about children who had been attending school irregularly; recently the education welfare officer (e.w.o.) had also been helpful in investigating other welfare problems involving family upsets that were having repercussions at school. After the e.w.o., the school nurse and school doctor were the most frequent visitors, though the head regretted that the doctor could only manage one visit a month. The educational psychologist did not visit at regular intervals but would always come at short notice if Joe gave him a ring, and the same applied to the school's general adviser. Social services were more of a problem. To his irritation, Joe found himself unable to establish a close informal relationship with any one social worker. The problem was partly that none of them seemed to stay long, but mainly that a family in the school's catchment area might be allocated to any one of a dozen social workers, depending on the exact address and whether the service had originally become involved in connection with the child or with one of his parents.

Joe Gardiner's personal relationship with outside agencies was bought at a price. Part of the price was his own time, which he did not grudge as he placed the welfare of the school's least successful and least privileged pupils near the top of his list of priorities. Another part of the price was that his class teachers did not have adequate opportunities to discuss children with the e.w.o., doctor or psychologist. The procedure was for the teacher to discuss the problem with the head and for the head to discuss it with the visiting expert. After making his or her inquiries the "expert" would tell the head what he had found, occasionally make recommendations and depart, leaving the head to report back to the class teacher.

It was a well-established system; as noted already it had helped to give the school a reputation for high standards of care towards less able or less privileged pupils. Joe Gardiner felt a mild sense of irritation, therefore, when he found it under attack both from his own staff and from the outside agencies themselves.

The first minor irritation had come when a new educational psychologist insisted on spending half a morning in the classroom and talking with the class teacher before seeing a child. The second came when he found that two other class teachers had discussed children with the psychologist informally during the lunch hour. He was pacified by the psychologist's assurance that naturally she would never see a child unless the head referred him formally.

A similar issue arose when the school doctor came back from a fortnight's course insisting that she too should see the class teacher. If a teacher suspected some medical problem or wanted advice about the educational implications of something that had already been diagnosed, for example slight hearing loss or short-sightedness, it was illogical to relay messages through the head. Then the e.w.o. jumped on the band-wagon − or at least two of his class teachers did, by button-holing the e.w.o. on his way to the head's office and telling him about two children whose attendance had been irregular.

The head's irritation at all these unorthodox developments was slightly modified by his reluctant recognition that they were probably both logical and desirable. As head his job was to set up a system, not to operate it himself. On the other hand, he also felt uneasy at not knowing what was happening. The rate things were going he would be having parents complaining about visits and inquiries he had never sanctioned.

The obvious solution was to hold a co-ordinating meeting once a week. Class teachers would be encouraged to discuss children informally with the e.w.o., psychologist and doctor, but no decision should be taken for a child or his parents to be offered a formal appointment unless it had first been agreed at the weekly welfare meeting. Joe also intended to use the meeting for general discussion about pupils whose work or behaviour was giving cause for concern. Apart from himself, the meeting was to be attended by his deputy, Dick Redman, the school's e.w.o., Eileen Peters, and any other teacher who wished to discuss any child's problems.

It would be held in the lunch hour on Thursday from 1.00−1.30 p.m. so that all teachers could, with a bit of effort make themselves available if necessary. Dick Redman had objected to holding the meeting in the lunch hour as he always stayed in his classroom at this time for children from his own and other classes to play draughts, draw or just talk. Some of the children who came were too timid to enjoy the playground and others had decided that his room was their safest way to avoid being blamed for something they had not done − or even that they had done. Dick was in a minority of one, though and was over-ruled.

The general concensus was that the meetings were a success. The e.w.o. felt more closely involved in the life and problems of the school and this increased her sense of commitment to it. The teachers now felt they had a regular forum to air problems informally; the exchange of views was to everyone's benefit. The head was glad of the regular opportunity to float his ideas informally and frequently advised his staff to have an informal word with the psychologist or the doctor, and report back if they thought that anything more formal was required. The psychologist and the doctor were also impressed by their easier, more frequent discussions with class teachers. Croft House's reputation for co-operative relationships with external agencies stood as high as ever.

The only cloud on the generally sunny horizon was a third year boy called Timothy Young. Timothy had already been discussed twice at the weekly meeting, and Eileen Peters had volunteered to make a home visit to see if his parents knew of anything that might be unsettling him. His parents did not know of anything, but the e.w.o. had suggested dryly that it just might have something to do with the fact that the electricity was cut off and the gas board were threatening similar action.

The first two times his name arose at the weekly meeting had been because of his poor educational progress and his generally unsettled behaviour. The third time was for something more serious. He had provoked a fight with another boy in the lunch hour and after throwing the other boy onto the ground, kicked him in the face knocking out two teeth. This sort of thing was not part of the accepted ethos at Croft House and Joe Gardiner had promptly excluded Timothy from school pending discussion with his parents about his future education.

Both parents had come in the following morning, extremely upset and desperately anxious that Mr Gardiner should have their son back. He told them he would consider the matter with his colleagues at the weekly welfare meeting, but that provided the Youngs were willing to accept help from the authority's psychological service he was willing to try to persuade them.

The staff were not averse to Timothy returning, though his class teacher suggested that it should be regarded as a "last chance"; if he did anything like this again, he should automatically be referred to a special school, she argued. Joe Gardiner pointed out that Timothy had already been referred to the educational psychologist. As head teacher he could request special education, but before making a decision the office would consult the doctor and the educational psychologist.

So far Dick Redman had been silent, but now he spoke for the first time. "May I just point out", he asked mildly, "that this incident occurred last Thursday? Timothy Young has been in my room every lunch hour for the last four weeks, except on Thursdays. Is this meeting in danger of becoming counter-productive?"

Questions

1 From the point of view of members of the support services, what were the advantages in the original system at Croft House?

2 How is a school's reputation made? In the case of Croft House, do you think the support services liked the school because of an objective

assessment of its achievements or because they were welcomed by the head?

3 Is there any way round the problem of erratic communication with the local social services department?

4 From a head teacher's point of view, what are the possible problems that could arise from outside agencies working directly with class teachers?

5 From a class teacher's point of view what are the possible advantages of outside agencies working only through the head teacher?

6 Is is true that the head's job is "to set up a system, not to operate it himself"?

7 Do you agree that the weekly co-ordinating meeting was "the obvious solution"? What other possibilities might have been considered?

8 Do you think the broader purpose of the meeting was necessary? Can general discussion about pupils whose work or behaviour gives cause for concern take place informally over coffee in the staff room?

9 There is a danger of this sort of meeting being successful for the first few months, but gradually "running out of steam". How might its usefulness be maintained?

10 The e.w.o. had agreed to see Timothy's parents, even though he was not an attendance problem. At your school, is the e.w.o. involved with general "welfare" cases, or is he/she only asked to help over attendance? Is it logical to confine the e.w.o.'s service to attendance?

11 Do you agree that Timothy should have been re-admitted?

12 The head implies that a direct request to the office for special education would be inappropriate, since the office would automatically contact the educational psychologist, who already knew Timothy. How do you think decisions regarding special schooling should be made?

13 Do you accept the decision that the weekly meeting was the cause of the problem? Can you think of times at your own school when meetings (or other policy decisions) have caused more problems than they have solved?

Dean

Main themes
1 Whether or not a child is considered ESN(M) depends not only on the child, but on the skills, and attitudes, of his teacher.
2 Parental attempts to help may aggravate problems that are already facing a child at school due to his teacher's attitudes and methods.

Joe Gardiner did not quite know how to start putting the educational psychologist in the picture about Dean Kirby. Dean's teacher was quite clear about the problem: "He's just ESN!" (Educationally Sub-Normal), she had told the weekly welfare meeting. "He shouldn't be here; it's not fair to him and it's not fair to the other children." Miss Arnold, though, was a teacher whose judgement was uncomplicated by such nebulous concepts as doubt. When her mind was made up, the head reflected wearily, nothing could shift her.

Dean was indeed dull. His progress had been slow since he started school but in the infant classes he had not stood out from five or six other children whose progress was, if anything, even slower than his own. His first junior school year had seen a slight deterioration. His progress continued, but more slowly and more erratically, and teachers started to notice that he looked tired and anxious. Things only came to a head in his second year in the juniors when he found himself in Miss Arnold's class.

In many ways Miss Arnold was an experienced teacher who often noticed things that other teachers had overlooked. She noticed, for example, that Dean's eye movements when he was reading were jerky and erratic at best; more often they seemed to be completely random. Miss Arnold would have given a brighter child some extra practice in visual sequencing to help him acquire the consistent left–right orientation required in reading English. Unfortunately she thought Dean too dull to benefit from anything so esoteric.

The impression of dullness was heightened by Dean's nervousness, timidity, tearfulness and rather shabby clothes. Temperamentally he had always been a retiring boy, sensitive to criticism from adults or other children, unwilling to assert himself. Miss Arnold did not like "spineless" children. Boys or girls whose aggressive, disruptive behaviour had reduced less experienced teachers to a state of near despair settled happily – and uncowed – into her class. In contrast, children who were cowed to start with usually stayed cowed. She had no skill in drawing a withdrawn child out of his shell.

Miss Arnold summed Dean up as a dull boy who needed skilled remedial teaching of the sort only a special school could provide. His dullness was aggravated by his over-sensitive disposition, she told the Thursday meeting. To her unconcealed irritation the head proposed that the education welfare officer (e.w.o.) should visit the parents to find out their views on Dean's progress, and if possible sound them out on the possibility of seeking advice from the psychological service.

Eileen Peters, the e.w.o., thought it would be more profitable to discuss her visit to the Kirbys with the head than with Miss Arnold. Mr Kirby, she told him, was a chronic invalid suffering from emphysema. He had drawn an invalidity pension for the last ten years. More important, he bitterly regretted his own lack of educational opportunities as a child and was determined that Dean should do better in life. He was quite obviously extremely anxious about his son's progress and was putting great pressure on him. Each night Dean had to read to his father. Apparently the sessions usually ended with the boy in tears and his father shouting at him for not trying. Mrs Kirby was a small retiring woman who busied herself around the home seemingly oblivious to the tension between father and son.

"They're in a vicious circle", Eileen said gloomily. "Dean's father was over-ambitious for him in the first place, but his difficulties have heightened his dad's anxieties and now these are being communicated to Dean who becomes less and less able to please his father with good progress in his reading as he becomes more and more anxious." Joe Gardiner already knew some of this and privately suspected that he ought to have called in the educational psychologist at least a year ago; she was good at persuading parents to put less pressure on their children.

Had Dean's teacher been anyone other than Miss Arnold, the head would by now have had little doubt about the need to ask that Dean be considered for special education. Previous experience, though, had taught him to treat her judgement with caution. The very qualities that made her successful with emotionally more outgoing children made her unsuccessful with boys like Dean. She did nothing by halves and once her mind was made up, nothing would induce her to change it. Her teaching methods might be old-fashioned but they undoubtedly worked for the majority. With children like Dean they simply seemed rigid, inflexible. Unless Miss Arnold's interest was aroused, reading consisted of a dreary, erratic progress through a scheme which she – along with half the infant teachers in the authority – had used for the last twenty years. Neither the language nor the characters in these books could possibly be expected to encourage anything but boredom or despair in a child who had already been failing to learn to read for five years.

Joe Gardiner felt no pride as these thoughts passed through his mind. He disliked the popular reading scheme in use in the infants department of his school, but the teachers liked it – or at least they had no wish to change – and he could not really complain about the results. By the time they reached the junior section of the school, all but a small minority had progressed beyond the need for any formal reading scheme. Until two years ago, a part-time teacher had taken the minority for remedial reading sessions. Abandoning what she called "the jerk-jerk chatter" of the infants' reading schemes, she based her sessions on her own assessment of each child's weaknesses and selected books or other materials accordingly. Unfortunately, the school had lost her in the last round of financial cuts and now backward readers had to take their chance in their ordinary classes. Some teachers were imaginative and conscientious; others were neither. With some children Miss Arnold was extraordinarily imaginative and conscientious. With a few others, she was neither.

During her home visit Eileen Peters had suggested to Mr and Mrs Kirby that the psychologist who visited Croft House School might see Dean in order to advise his teachers what they could best do to help him. They were therefore, anxious, but not surprised when Dean brought a letter home from school inviting them to meet the psychologist at 3.00 p.m. the next day. They turned up in their smartest clothes to find the psychologist had spent the morning watching Dean's work in the classroom and the first part of the afternoon seeing Dean on his own.

She had guessed — quite correctly — that the interview would be a difficult one. As it progressed she found she had to do two, almost mutually exclusive things: first she had to explain to both parents that Dean was a far from intelligent little boy who needed skilled remedial teaching; and second she had to persuade Mr Kirby that his own anxious efforts to help Dean were counter-productive. "But he's not getting on at school so someone has to give him something extra", objected Mr Kirby at once. The psychologist agreed patiently, and asked Mr Kirby if he had ever thought Dean might benefit from a spell in a special school with smaller classes and teachers who could give individual attention. At first he was, as Joe Gardiner had predicted, horrified by the idea. In the end, however, he agreed to visit the nearby special school.

"It's difficult to know whether this recommendation is justified", the psychologist admitted to the head later that afternoon. "Dean is a dull boy, but no duller than half a dozen other children in the school. He has got specific learning difficulties, but so do most of the others. The state he's in at the moment is partly due to his own lack of ability, but it's also due to the fact that he's a vulnerable child temperamentally; that his father has nothing to do except worry about him; and that Miss Arnold has made up her mind that he's ESN. I don't know which of these is most important, and I understand your point that you couldn't ask the teachers of either of the two parallel classes to accept yet another problem child. Personally I think he will be happier at the special school, but I don't think it will make much difference to his educational progress. For what it's worth, the research suggests that ESN(M) children make better progress at ordinary schools, even though they may be happier in special education."

Questions

1 Have you ever felt as sure about a child as Miss Arnold felt about Dean? Did you have more justification?

2 In your experience is it possible to tell in advance which of half a dozen equally dull children will eventually "make the grade", and which will still be floundering in two years' time? If you think you can predict, *how* do you do so?

3 Could Miss Arnold be justified in not giving Dean specific remedial help on the grounds that he was too dull to benefit? What remedial help might the special school have given him that Miss Arnold was unwilling (rather than unable) to provide?

4 Are you particularly sympathetic to, or successful with, children with particular personalities, aptitudes or difficulties? How has your own background influenced your attitudes and skills?

5 Can you think of children from your own class who have been under pressure at home because their parents regretted their own lack of educational opportunity? What can you as a class teacher do about this?

6 Give other examples of children who find themselves in a vicious circle.

7 Write the script of an interview in which you, as a teacher, try to persuade a worried and ambitious parent to put less pressure on his child.

8 Describe a personality clash between you and a child in your class, and explain what you did to reduce the problems caused by your and the child's feelings about each other.

9 Do you agree that neither the language nor the characters in some of the most widely-used reading schemes could be expected "to encourage anything but boredom or despair in a child who had already been failing to learn to read for five years"?

10 Do you agree that a core reading scheme is needed in an infant class?

11 What pressure might the head have put on Miss Arnold?

12 Do you agree with the educational psychologist's assessment of the reasons for the state Dean was in when she saw him?

13 Have any children from your classes gone to special schools? Have you followed up their progress?

Blackstone Middle School

Main themes

1 Routine testing is an unimaginative, time-consuming exercise which often fails to provide the information that teachers need.

2 Inadequate attention is often paid to the readability of books used in the classroom.

3 If you know the reading age assumed by the books available to children, the need for individual testing is greatly reduced.

Harold Jowitt, the head of Blackstone Middle School was not one of those people who believe that if a job is worth doing, it is worth doing badly. He prided himself on tackling things one at a time and making a thorough job of them. Last year he had concentrated on the teaching of maths throughout the school. He had been right in identifying this as a weak link; indeed it was depressingly obvious that most of his staff had disliked the subject as children, disliked teaching it and were transferring their own dislike onto their present pupils. The authority's maths adviser had laid on a course for all staff on four consecutive Wednesday lunchtimes, and this was followed up with evening workshops based at the school and at the Teachers' Centre with colleagues from neighbouring schools. The interest and enthusiasm was reflected in the children's work and had already drawn a favourable comment from the head of the maths department at the local comprehensive school.

This year Harold Jowitt planned to review the arrangements for monitoring pupil's progress in reading and identifying the children who needed extra help. The system for the last few years had been for every child to be given Schonell's Graded Word Reading Test once a year. The 20 per cent whose reading age was furthest behind their chronological age went to Hilary Marshal, who withdrew them from their ordinary classes in groups of about ten for remedial reading.

Hilary had been complaining about this system ever since she took on the remedial post two years earlier. The first year the head had put her off on the grounds that it was French year, and the second that it was maths year. Next year, he told her, it would be her turn. Her reasons for objecting to the existing procedures were straightforward enough. She was the person expected to carry out the annual review of reading ages and it seemed an almost total waste of time.

The limitations of any graded word reading test were well known, she pointed out to the head. Such tests only measured a child's ability to bark at words. They told the teacher nothing about his ability to understand the written word, nor about his ability to read with sufficient fluency for enjoyment and meaning. She cited several children who achieved quite good scores on Schonell's Graded Word Reading Test yet were obviously failing in their classroom work. Just as serious, teachers were unable to relate the results to anything except national norms which were hopelessly out of date.

She pointed out that at least two of the fourth year classes were struggling because some of their text books required too high a reading level. Harold Jowitt accepted this point but thought it was logically distinct from the problem of recording each child's progress each year. Hilary persisted with her argument that test results were pointless, if not meaningless, if they bore no relationship to what was taught in the classroom and the head had eventually agreed to make the following year "testing and remedial reading year".

A co-ordinating group was set up consisting of the head, Hilary, the deputy head, Harry Williams, and a class teacher, Kaye Maxfield. Their first step was to determine the scope of the review. This they summarised under four headings: (i) investigation of ways to record children's progress in word recognition and higher-level reading skills; (ii) assessment of the accuracy of the match between the reading level assumed by books in use in each classroom and the children's actual reading ability; (iii) the assessment of children with reading problems and the reasons for these problems; (iv) using the results of assessment in planning future work with each child, both in the classroom and in the remedial reading sessions.

They ran into an immediate problem when the head and Kaye Maxfield both argued that annual assessment should be carried out by someone independent, not the class teacher. Hilary argued that they were pre-judging the issue by talking about annual assessment. If teachers kept adequate records themselves, the annual testing ritual would become redundant. They started therefore, by thinking about the reading level assumed by the books in use in the classroom and the children's actual ability.

"The trouble is that we can't match the two except by using the Schonell reading ages we've already got", objected Harry Williams, "and we are all agreed that those are inadequate." Hilary patiently explained the method for measuring the reading age assumed by a book which involves selecting words at random and counting the number of syllables in each. "You see", she said, "if we involve all the teachers in the exercise we can build up a picture of the reading age required for every book in the school. It's then possible to select certain books and make up our own test to assess the children's accuracy and comprehension of each book."

If Harold Jowitt had thought that "testing and remedial reading year" would be an anti-climax after maths year he was rapidly coming to a different conclusion. Hilary explained in detail the assessment of a text's reading level and how the readability tests were carried out. His interest aroused, Harold Jowitt became enthusiastic. "It's a completely new approach to testing", he exclaimed, "and we could use it to colour mark all the books in the library too, so that the children can look at the spine and see at a glance whether they will be able to read and understand it. Only today I was in the library and three second year girls were struggling with something that was obviously too difficult for them. We could have a colour chart in each classroom, showing what reading level each child has progressed to."

Colour marking each book according to reading level took the rest of the Autumn term and most of the Easter term. It provided a number of surprises, notably that the reading level in some of the maths and some primary science material varied widely from page to page. The authors just did not seem to have had any idea what reading age they were writing for. The exercise also led to a re-appraisal of some of the books in use in most classrooms. Several proved too difficult for over half the children, and a smaller proportion seemed, in spite of the blurb, to be aimed at a younger age group.

When they progressed to consideration of the assessment of children with reading problems they found they had already covered part of this with the colour coding system. This would show at a glance which children were seriously backward and which children had made unsatisfactory progress in the course of the year. They ran into disagreement when the head and Kaye Maxfield thought it essential to know which children were failing because of some specific learning difficulty and which were backward because of general intellectual dullness. In other words, they wanted to match intelligence with attainment.

Hilary was unenthusiastic. More important than knowing who had a high or average IQ and who had a low IQ, was understanding the nature of the difficulties the child experienced when reading. If he had sequencing difficulties it did not much matter whether he was bright or dull as far as his remedial programme was concerned. She had two further arguments. First, the research on the effects of remedial reading showed that progress was not closely associated with IQ. Second, other research had compared the progress of backward readers whose reading level was not all that much behind the level predicted from their IQ, with the progress of retarded readers whose reading was retarded relative to their IQ. The results had not been related to remedial provision, but showed that the retarded readers had a *worse* outlook. "But I don't know whether that proves we should be helping the retarded children who have the worse outlook or the backward ones who have a better outlook", Hilary concluded. The others accepted her view that intellectual assessment was not needed.

They did think, however, that individual diagnostic testing would be useful for children who were obviously making unsatisfactory progress. Having previously looked at a number of group tests, they agreed on the Neale Analysis of Reading Ability, with Daniels and Diack's Standard Reading Tests as a back-up if more complex visuo-perceptual problems were suspected.

Questions

1 Can a teacher afford to be a perfectionist? Is it not often the case that a job worth doing is worth doing badly?

2 What arguments do you see for and against the head's policy of tackling curriculum reform at one subject a year?

3 What are other limitations in the use of graded word reading tests to identify backward readers?

4 Is a group of ten realistic for a remedial session? Would you prefer a smaller group meeting less often, or a larger one more often?

5 Can you think of children from your own class who achieved good word-recognition scores on a graded word test, yet were obviously failing on comprehension test?

6 Does a graded word test really measure only the ability to "bark at print"?

7 Can you think of books in regular use in your classroom which are written at an unsuitable reading level for your pupils?

8 Is Hilary Marshal right in regarding the results of tests as "pointless, if not meaningless" if they bear no relationship to what is taught in class?

9 Are you happy with the scope of the review of testing and remedial work?

10 Do you agree with the view that annual assessment should not need to be carried out by someone independent, but by the class teacher?

11 Explain how to assess the readability of any book you are currently using. Use the assessment with your class.

12 Do you think the colour marking system proposed here is accurate enough?

13 Do you agree with Hilary Marshal's doubts about the usefulness of intellectual assessment? What are the dangers in this?

14 In practice, can a colour marking system be used to record children's progress? What follow-up and future guidance would be needed for teachers to use this successfully?

15 What other tests might be used in assessing the nature of specific reading difficulties? What are the strengths and limitations of the two tests suggested?

Nicholas

Main themes

1 Taking too much interest in "disturbed" behaviour can have the effect of encouraging it.
2 Intellectual assessment can yield severely misleading results.

3 For many "maladjusted" children the best form of treatment is placement in a well-run class in an ordinary school.

Nicholas Purcell joined Blackstone Middle School because the authority's administrative officers were slow on the uptake. His family moved into the area during the summer holiday and his father wrote to the office requesting his admission to Blackstone Middle School. Normally the request would have been a mere formality, but Nick's previous school had been a special school for maladjusted children. Mr Purcell had pointed this out in his letter to the office but had made clear: (i) that his son had never been formally ascertained under the 1944 Education Act, and (ii) that he wished him to be placed in an ordinary school.

Due to the summer holidays (or, less charitably, to inefficiency, the head thought) the letter was still unanswered the day before the new term started. Mr Purcell therefore visited the office to find out what was happening about his son's future education. A harrassed clerk told him that inquiries were still being made, but Mr Purcell insisted that term began tomorrow and he wanted confirmation that his son could start at Blackstone Middle School. The clerk insisted this was quite out of the question in view of Nick's previous special school history. Mr Purcell promptly demanded to know where he could contact Councillor Dale, the Chairman of the Education Committee. The clerk hurried away to find a senior assistant education officer, and fifteen minutes later Mr Purcell was leaving the building with a promise that Nicholas might start at Blackstone, "on trial and subject to the reports we receive from his last education authority" the official told him firmly.

Now nine years old, Nick had spent the last three years in special education. He had been placed when he became out of control in his infants school. His difficult behaviour was undoubtedly related largely to his mother deserting the family rather suddenly, leaving his father to cope with Nicholas and the two younger children. It may also have had something to do with the fact that his teacher had an anxious, nervous manner similar to his mother's. Struggling to keep the family together, Mr Purcell had felt in no position to oppose the recommendation.

Eighteen months later Mr Purcell married Nicholas' stepmother, a widow with two girls of her own, one older and one younger than Nick. There had been a difficult twelve months but the family was now feeling relatively settled. Nick still tended to provoke his stepmother but not with the same intensity. He was also starting to play with his brothers and stepsisters, though he still liked to dominate.

At first Mr Purcell had been relieved at Nick's removal to the special school but after a few months he became increasingly puzzled by Nick's stories of events at school. The children were allowed to swear, some of them even hit the teachers! Mr Purcell's own visits to the school did little to relieve his anxiety. The teachers were invariably welcoming, and quite obviously had the children's welfare at heart. Yet Mr Purcell found the casual atmosphere hard to accept. He admitted that the children did seem to be doing some work — examples were stuck up all over the corridors — but he was unhappy about his son's progress.

If he had seen his son's behaviour at the school he would have been unhappier still. The aggressive, angry little boy on admission had disappeared. In his place there was a wheedling, immature child with an excessively dependent relationship on his female class teacher. In her absence he would sit on the floor under a table, thumb in mouth, rocking and moaning and resisting all kindly efforts to coax him out. The school's visiting psychiatrist called it a fascinating example of regression and maintained a close interest in the case.

Although Mr Purcell knew nothing of this behaviour, he and his second wife both decided that Nick's stay at special school had outlived its usefulness. The family's move to a new house and a new school authority seemed the obvious time for a return to normality.

Nick caused quite a stir on his first day at Blackstone. Ignoring all convention about social distance he went up to his class teacher, Kaye Maxfield when she called him to her desk and leant against her in the friendly way he used to lean against his teacher at his special school. Kaye pushed him away indignantly, so Nick promptly crawled under her desk, put his thumb in his mouth and started rocking. The rest of the class gaped, speechless and bewildered for a moment before becoming noisily indignant. Kaye, too was speechless for a moment, then recovered herself to pull Nick unceremoniously out by his feet, yank him to a standing position and tell him in a loud, angry voice that children didn't behave like that at Blackstone Middle School. She sent him back to his desk, then told him to try coming to her desk again.

Thoroughly chastened, Nick behaved perfectly for the rest of the day. In fact, he behaved almost perfectly for the rest of the week, and the week after. There was a bit of bragging in the playground, but he quickly discovered that the other children were unimpressed. Being an oddity just wasn't any fun!

A month after the beginning of term, Kaye was more concerned about Nick's reading than about his behaviour. He seemed to be an exception to the general rule in that his comprehension appeared to be in advance of his word-recognition skills. Although he frequently found himself unable to read individual words, he was often able to grasp the general gist.

It was therefore with some surprise that Kaye read the report of the special school psychologist. The senior assistant education officer had written to his opposite number in Nick's previous authority immediately after Mr Purcell's visit, asking for information about Nick and advice about his future educational needs. The opposite number had passed the inquiry to the educational psychologist who reported that she had seen Nick for a routine review only three months earlier. "Before admission to the special school he was in too disturbed a state to test", she wrote, "but my most recent assessment shows him to be a dull boy with an IQ of 67 on the revised version of the Wechsler Intelligence Scale for Children. He has made some progress here but remains an extremely immature, dependent little boy who badly needs the continual support of a female teacher with whom he has developed a close relationship. His reading age on a graded word recognition test is only 7.0; if he were remaining at his old address I would certainly not have considered a change of school desirable, but in view of his family's recent move I suggest he would be appropriately placed in a school for ESN(M) (Educationally Sub-Normal (Moderate) children, or perhaps a school which can cater for pupils who are both ESN(M) and maladjusted."

The administrator enclosed Form SE1 with this report, so that Mr Jowitt might complete it as a formal request for Nicholas' trial at Blackstone to be concluded. The only snag was that neither Kaye Maxfield nor Hilary Marshal, who had just started to assess Nick's reading problems, saw any need to conclude the trial. "That report's not worth the paper it's written on. The IQ figure must be wrong. At least, if it's not, at least half a dozen other children in my class are ESN(M)", Kaye said irritably. Hilary was just as emphatic. "He just hasn't been taught any of the more complex phonic rules, it's not surprising his word recognition is so poor. There's absolutely no problem of comprehension — it's a simple question of filling in a few gaps in his knowledge of phonics. There must be twenty children in the school whose reading I am more worried about."

Before replying to the a.e.o.'s letter the head asked the Purcells to come to the school. Satisfied that they were happy with their son's progress and had no wish for him to re-enter a special school, Harold Jowitt wrote the a.e.o. a polite note thanking him for his helpful suggestion and explaining that as Nick had made an encouraging start neither he, nor his staff nor the Purcells wished to pursue the matter at the moment.

Questions

1 What is meant by formal ascertainment under the 1944 Education Act?

2 Could the authority insist on placing Nick in a special school?

3 Do you think Mr Purcell would have got a similar reception if he had visited the office of your own authority?

4 The implication is that Mr Purcell's request was granted because he was articulate and well-informed. Do you think children are sometimes moved to special schools largely because their parents are not?

5 Nick's infant school teacher had the same temperament as his mother. Can you think of instances where a child has proved difficult with a particular teacher because the teacher reminded him of a parent or relation? Can you think of children with whom the reverse has happened?

6 If Nick was correct in telling his parents children could swear at his special school, can you justify this?

7 How might the special school have relieved the Purcells'anxiety about Nick's progress?

8 How do you think the psychiatrist (and teachers) interpreted Nick's dependent relationship with his special school class teacher?

9 How do you think they interpreted his rocking and moaning? Do you agree with them?

10 Would you have reacted in the same way as Kaye Maxfield to Nick's behaviour on his first day at Blackstone Middle School?

11 What other factors might have influenced the psychologist in reaching her decision? Do you agree that it was a mistaken one?

12 Can you think of cases where psychologists' reports have been similarly mistaken?

13 Do you agree that Nick's reading problems could have been due simply to inadequate teaching at his special school?

14 What are the other possible explanations?

15 How could the special school legitimately defend its work with Nick?

Hill Top Primary School

Main themes

1 Persuading l.e.a.s. to give extra resources depends more on the people whose support you enlist and on the way you submit your request than on the nature of the request itself.

2 "Remedial" education does not just involve the formal curriculum.

Clive Braddock's request for an additional member of staff had not been taken too seriously in County Hall. He was already fully staffed and although Hill Top Primary School had a difficult catchment area, no one felt inclined to make out a special case for him.

Yet the head thought he had made out a special case on two grounds. The first was a combination of his school's size and its catchment area. Easily the authority's largest primary school, with nearly 600 children including the nursery department with 50 children attending part-time, the buildings had originally served as an old board elementary school, then as a secondary modern following the 1944 Education Act, and had only reverted to their present use as a primary school when the authority re-organised secondary education on a comprehensive system and built an extensive new block adjacent to the former grammar school. The classrooms at Hill Top were roomy – or barn-like depending on your point of view – with tall narrow windows that stopped six feet from the floor. Unfortunately, there were not enough classrooms, so the infants department was housed in a mobile classroom in one of the school yards and four other infant classes occupied "relocatable" buildings, which were only slightly more permanent, in another.

Apart from a small Roman Catholic voluntary school, Hill Top Primary was the only school to serve two of the largest housing estates in the city. The area did not suffer from inner-city blight and most of the families were well-established. Nevertheless the lack of social mix was reflected in the poor provision of amenities in the area and little use of what amenities did exist. Last year the district council had thankfully shelved ambitious plans for a new library after hearing evidence that the present library was under-used. No one who knew the

69

present library, with its limited range of books and its depressing mid-Victorian building was surprised by its under-use.

In applying for an extra teacher on his staff Mr Braddock had made three points. First, he had been slightly under-staffed all the previous year. Although the appointment of a part-time teacher now meant his staffing level was up to, but not above his establishment, he argued that the complexities of the school site with its scatter of outbuildings justified additional support. Second, the school had seven teachers in their probationary year or only their second year of teaching; in most parts of the city this might not matter but the problems in Hill Top's catchment area created severe difficulties for inexperienced teachers and they needed more support than it was possible to give them. Finally, there were the problems presented by the children themselves. Mr Braddock had carried out a survey the previous term in which the class teachers completed a Rutter B(2) Scale on each child. The results of this behaviour questionnaire, claimed the head, showed that 25 per cent of all children were showing signs of severe emotional and behavioural disorder.

Although County Hall did not appear to take Clive Braddock's letter too seriously, his managers showed more than a passing interest. The results of his questionnaire led to heated discussion at their termly meeting, following which a resolution was passed urging the chief education officer to re-consider the problems outlined in the head's original application and to advise them on possible solutions.

The weak point in Mr Braddock's application had been his failure to specify how he would use the proposed extra teacher. As the school's general adviser pointed out, simply creating an extra class would not make much difference in a school of Hill Top's size, and in any case he had no classroom to spare. Clive's intention had been to use the teacher in two ways. First, he wanted his deputy to take on more responsibility, including support for probationer teachers; if the deputy could be relieved for half his timetable it would create a breathing space. Second, he wanted one of his other teachers to take remedial groups. Thus the new teacher would take the deputy's class in the mornings and the class of the prospective remedial teacher in the afternoons.

The adviser was sceptical. Did Clive not remember the situation when he took over the school five years earlier and the deputy was not taking a class at all? Even allowing for the previous head's illness, the results of that experience hardly suggested he was the ideal person to support probationers. The adviser had another criticism. The results of the survey had demonstrated that a high proportion of children were showing behaviour problems. He accepted that behaviour problems and learning difficulties overlapped, but doubted very much whether a part-time remedial class was the way to tackle a child's emotional difficulties. "Certainly giving them successful experiences in school will build up their confidence out of school", he argued, "but aren't you putting the cart before the horse? If, as you claim, the children's problems arise from stress at home, shouldn't you be setting up something which tries to compensate for this stress?"

The theory seemed alright but the possibility of converting it into practice more doubtful. The head had, however, noticed a circular in his weekly bundle

70

of papers from the office about a forthcoming conference on special units. He had not read it carefully at the time but looking at it again he saw that two sessions were dealing with "nurture groups" in infant schools and "adjustment groups" in primary schools.

Before attending the conference he telephoned the school's educational psychologist to find out more about this approach. She gave him four articles which described how the groups were set up and what they were trying to do. He made two more telephone calls, this time asking the adviser and the chairman of his managers to join him and the educational psychologist at the conference.

A month later the managers endorsed a revised letter of application for two part-time members of staff, one to work with the infants department and one with the juniors. The infant teacher would run a nurture group, the point of which would be to ease the transition from home to school for a number of pupils who experienced great difficulty in settling. The atmosphere would be informal, with the emphasis on providing an experience of consistent attention from a warm, stable adult which these children had missed before starting school. The head of the infants department had written, "There are some children who cannot benefit from the educational experiences we have to offer until they have learnt to accept and to give in their play with other children, to trust an adult to behave with warmth and consistency, and to trust themselves to risk failure by trying something new. This applies especially to children from problem families who did not come to our nursery. The aim of the nurture group would be to provide in a smaller, more intensive group, some of the opportunities for social learning which we wish the children had been given at nursery school and at home."

The teacher taking groups of juniors was to have a slightly different role. By this stage most children had found their feet, but in some cases adverse family conditions meant that they remained highly unsettled at school. The junior school's "adjustment groups" therefore aimed at providing attention and support for pupils whose poor attainments or disturbed behaviour might reflect pressures at home. Again the atmosphere would be informal; the emphasis would be on providing an opportunity for counselling in the course of activities which the children had themselves selected. The head wrote, "Every teacher knows that children show a different side of themselves in small groups. Taking a small group frequently gives the teacher an understanding of the child's personality and of his problems outside school which was previously lacking and which can only help in his future teaching. The proposed groups would not only offer children the support and interest of a warm, stable adult figure, but would also provide an opportunity to help them learn socially more constructive patterns of behaviour."

The groups were to be based in two small rooms in the main body of the school. One was a converted stock cupboard and the other had been used as a language room until the school had stopped teaching French two years ago. Each group would operate on a half-time basis. The nurture group would take the same six or seven children every day, but it was expected that the adjustment groups would withdraw children from their ordinary lessons only for one or two sessions a week. Both groups would be monitored by the authority's psychological and advisory services.

A fortnight later the adviser telephoned Clive Braddock. "Don't quote me", he said, "but I think we can swing it. There have been three problems; one or two people are frightened that word will get round and lead to a flood of applications; there are one or two others who think that the nurture groups don't sound all that much different from a good infant class, except in size; they also think it would be better to help with the adjustment group children by giving additional support in the ordinary class rather than creating the sort of alternative to the classroom which you describe. Finally, I've had to persuade a few people that you are not out to compete with the special schools. I think we're overcoming these problems, though, and you should hear something soon."

Questions

1 Are there any advantages in a large primary school?

2 Are there any advantages in old buildings like those at Hill Top? How can the disadvantages be reduced by the teacher or overcome by structural alterations?

3 Can you think of other areas where facilities such as libraries are under-used? Is the under-use partly related to poor facilities, or is it wholly attributable to apathy and indifference in the local community?

4 Do buildings like those at Hill Top Primary School justify extra staffing?

5 The school had an exceptional number of probationer teachers. What are the possible reasons for this?

6 The head used the Rutter B(2) Scale to survey the children's behaviour problems. What other methods or techniques might he have used? Would they have been any more successful?

7 Is the number of pupils who show signs of emotional or behavioural disorder surprising, in view of what is known from other studies?

8 Were there any other weak points in the head's application? Do you agree with the adviser's criticisms?

9 Can you think of schools in which this summary of the children's problems by the head of the infant department would be valid? How would you tackle these problems with an ordinary class?

10 Do you agree with the implied differences in needs between infant and junior school pupils?

11 What are the limitations of the aims and methods described?

12 Do you see strong arguments against staffing groups of this sort with teachers who are not already on the staff?

13 Is there any validity in the doubts which the adviser had heard expressed by his colleagues at the office?

Cheryl

Main themes
1 Children who are neglected at home often behave aggressively at school – but the aggression may take unpredictable forms.

2 Some children's behaviour becomes more difficult as they start to feel more secure.

Cheryl Cope was the sort of child for whom the nurture group at Hill Top Primary School had been set up. Her mother brought her along on the first day of term, giving only the briefest word of explanation that she suffered from alopaecia. Mrs Cope had not accepted an invitation to visit the school with Cheryl the term before she started, nor did she respond to the school's first two requests to bring her daughter's birth certificate for the purpose of formal registration. She was very busy, she explained when she eventually brought it in following the third request, what with working from 9.30 until 5 o'clock and having the house to look after as well.

Cheryl was the oldest of two girls. Father was a long-distance lorry driver, often away from home. Mother worked as a machinist in a factory. Before starting school both girls had been looked after during the day by one of the many unregistered child-minders in the district. Indeed, Cheryl returned to the same child-minder from school in the afternoon until her mother got home from the factory. For the first few days the child-minder had collected her at the gate, but subsequently Cheryl joined the group of other infant class children and their mums to be shown across the road by the lollipop man, and found her own way. It was only four minutes walk, with no other main roads to cross.

Cheryl was well-clothed and always had money for her school dinners. She stood out for three reasons. First, and most immediately obvious, was the large bald patch on her head and the thin, dry look of what hair she did have. Second, she tended to wet herself. It only happened once or twice a week, but six months after starting school there was no sign of any improvement. Finally, she seldom mixed with the other children and would only reply to the teacher in monosyllables. "Waif-like", her teacher commented in the staff room. After the first

73

three days her mother dropped her at the playground entrance in the morning and was not seen again.

The school medical officer saw all reception class children in the course of their first year. Mary Fort, Cheryl's class teacher, asked that she should be placed early on the list. At the first appointment neither parent turned up; at the second the child-minder turned up and was told that the doctor appreciated her taking the trouble to come, but it was the mother or father she needed to talk to; at the third, the mother arrived breathless and fifteen minutes late after missing the bus from the factory.

"I don't know what it's all about", she said as she caught her breath, "because we've had her to our own doctor and he says she will probably grow out of it given time." The school doctor had had a long day and was irritated by Mrs Cope's manner. "Grow out of what?" she demanded acidly, "her withdrawn, uncommunicative state, her wetting, or is it her alopaecia you are talking about?"

Mrs Cope glared at the doctor. "I meant her hair, of course", she mumbled, "what else do you mean?" Further questioning revealed: (i) that Cheryl's alopaecia had started when she was three years old, but had never been investigated by the hospital's consultant dermatologist; (ii) that Cheryl wet the bed every night and was occasionally wet in the day at week-ends; (iii) that Mrs Cope spanked her for this whenever it happened and then it didn't happen again that day; (iv) that she was defiant and stubborn at home; (v) that Mr Cope thought the world of Cheryl. "In fact much more than he thinks of me", said her mother resentfully.

The doctor asked Mrs Cope if she would like her to arrange an appointment for Cheryl at the hospital. Mrs Cope demurred, but agreed after pointing out that her GP had said it would probably clear up on its own. This turned out not to be strictly true. When the school doctor spoke to him on the telephone he said he had been concerned about Cheryl for a long time. He would gladly have referred her to a specialist but had been forced to agree when Mrs Cope pointed out that referral hadn't helped two other child patients of his who lived in the same street. "Actually", he added, "I'm not sure that a child psychiatrist wouldn't be better than a dermatologist, but you don't really need a psychiatrist to tell you that this mother has no time for her children." Nor inclination to find time, the school doctor thought bitterly — a suspicion that was strengthened when the hospital sent her a note saying that two appointments with the dermatologist had been missed without explanation and they were reluctantly closing the case.

Cheryl was placed in the nurture group a month after starting at Hill Top. An invitation to her mother to visit the school to discuss the move was not answered. Bessie Croft, the teacher in charge of the nurture group found at first that Cheryl faded into the background, watching but seldom participating, in the same way as she did in the classroom. After a few weeks a gradual change became apparent. Cheryl was slyly interfering in other children's activities. When they reacted she repeated the provocation, but if Bessie spoke to her she would cover her face in her hands and refuse to speak. "It strikes me", said Bessie in conversation with Mary Fort, Cheryl's regular teacher, "that this is a highly effective device from Cheryl's point of view. It not only gets grown-ups worried when they can't get children to speak; it makes them spend a lot of time with the child as well, and however angry you may feel you don't like to show it if the child seems upset and withdrawn."

The idea that Cheryl's withdrawn behaviour was her way of expressing the anger and resentment she felt, was a novel one which had not occurred to either teacher before. They realised, of course, that she probably had quite a lot to feel angry about in her treatment − or lack of it − at home, but were not used to feelings of resentment being expressed in this way. "It reminds me a bit of our next door neighbours", Mary Fort remarked thoughtfully. "They got themselves into a terrible state about their two-year-old's toilet training. He just sat on the potty refusing to do a thing and loving all the attention he got from his parents as they got more and more worried, and more and more angry!"

Whether this analogy was valid or not, it was certainly the case that Cheryl was coming out of her shell − or rather leaping out of it. First in the nurture group then in the regular classroom her sly disruption of other children's activities developed into open disruption. Her refusal to speak to her teacher developed into a more explicit form of defiance characterised by "won't" and "make me" or more often "you can't make me!" The nurture group activity she most enjoyed was cooking. Twice a week the children baked cakes for a small tea at the end of afternoon school. Cheryl was greedier than any of the other children, clamouring for another cup and often trying to persuade or threaten other children into parting with their cakes. Bessie Croft was reminded of the social training described in one of the articles the head had given her about nurture groups: "I see; I grab; I don't get!" The trouble was there were times when Cheryl *did* get!

In the classroom she did a minimum of work. Originally this had been because she was too withdrawn. Now she was too busy interrupting other children's work to do any of her own. Bessie and Mary were not sure whether to accept all this as an encouraging development in the hope that she would soon progress to a more stable pattern of behaviour, or to put more overt pressure on her to conform. They decided to put pressure on her because of the effect she was starting to have on other children. The pressure was simple. If Cheryl did not behave well enough with Mrs Fort she would have to miss her next session with Miss Croft.

"You realise, of course, that if she gets worse this means she'll be spending her whole week with you", the head of the infants department warned Mary. They thought it was worth the risk, reasoning that it was the only way they could resolve two conflicting needs: (i) Cheryl's need to express her feelings in the only way she knew how to express them, and (ii) the other children's need to get on with their work without disturbance. They also thought that if Cheryl did not learn to behave in a more normal, acceptable manner sooner rather than later, she might have to be considered for a special school. Her teachers thought that this might well be the right thing for her, but felt obliged to explore all other possibilities first.

Questions

1 What inquiries could the school have made when Mrs Cope failed to bring her daughter's birth certificate to school?

2 Is there any evidence that children are at risk from the mere fact of spending the day with a child-minder? Is a working mother necessarily a disadvantage?

3 Do you consider it acceptable for a five-year-old to find his own way home from school, even if home is only four minutes walk away with no main roads to cross?

4 How could the head teacher have arranged a medical examination at an earlier stage? Can such an examination be a legal requirement?

5 What is the likely effect of the school doctor's first question to Mrs Cope? Do you consider it was justified?

6 Is it unusual for a child of Cheryl's age to be wet every night?

7 What do you infer about Mrs Cope and about the family relationships from her interview with the doctor?

8 Could the doctor have alerted any other agencies to the stress Cheryl was under at home? Which ones? Would there have been any point if Mrs Cope did not wish to co-operate?

9 Is there any legal action open to the education department or any other statutory agency which might be: (i) possible and (ii) appropriate in a case like this?

10 Do you agree with Mary Fort's assessment of Cheryl's motive for not speaking? Have you taught children who could not be persuaded to talk? What did you think were the reasons?

11 Have you taught children who develop from a withdrawn state to an openly defiant one?

12 What are the different explanations for Cheryl's greediness?

13 Do you agree with Bessie Croft's and Mary Fort's plan of action? What other approaches might they have adopted?

14 Do you think Cheryl would be suitably placed in a special school? If so, what sort of special school? What would be the advantages and possible disadvantages of this course of action?

Stonerace Infants School

Main themes

1 To be of maximum value, compensatory – or remedial – education must be closely integrated into the child's day-to-day classroom activities.

2 Withdrawal groups are not the only – and often not the best – way to provide children and their teachers with additional help.

3 Part-time teachers may be able to make a greater contribution by sharing a class than by withdrawing groups for specific activities.

Miss Morgan had been head of Stonerace Infants School for three years now and had overcome the inevitable teething problems associated with the retirement of her much loved and respected predecessor. Her predecessor had also been much feared: "A heart of gold and a will of iron – woe betide any teacher, child, parent or local authority adviser who crosses her path", a new member of the advisory team had been warned by a colleague. The result was that the school operated smoothly and cheerfully on principles that the old head's many admirers happily called "old-fashioned".

Miss Morgan's appointment was based on the managers' belief that she would continue the old well-established principles, but introduce sufficient new ideas to keep the school up to date without indulging in new and untried experiments. This hope had been fulfilled. As was to be expected, some parents still hankered after the good old days but a greater number welcomed the more relaxed atmosphere and easier access to teachers. Most of the staff had stayed and they also seemed pleased with the new regime; after all, it was not so very different from the old one.

Yet there was one area that left Miss Morgan with a feeling of dissatisfaction. For the last ten years an elderly lady had spent each afternoon taking groups of the final year children for remedial reading. Miss Morgan was not unhappy about her results; they were good, even after allowing for the fact that she only accepted the brighter of the backward readers – the ones she thought were "ready to learn". Miss Morgan's objections were four-fold:

First, she did not think the children selected were the ones who most needed additional help. She thought they would probably do all right in the junior school whether they received extra help or not, whereas the more generally backward children who would certainly have to struggle to survive in their first junior school year were getting nothing extra.

Second, she thought that some of the younger children needed additional help more than some of the older ones who were receiving it; the additional help they needed was not remedial reading, though, but rather a language development programme to compensate for their previous lack of linguistic and educational experience in the broader sense.

Third, the class teachers only benefited indirectly from the remedial sessions, since there was no co-ordination between the remedial group work and the children's ordinary class work.

Fourth, she knew that some class teachers found it very difficult to give attention to the children who needed it most, the quiet, withdrawn ones who were easily overlooked. This was partly because they concentrated, understandably, on the more articulate majority, but in a few cases, because they spent all their energy controlling the disruptive effects of one or two exceptionally troublesome children.

As long as the old remedial teacher remained there was little hope of any change. "I've just got to wait for the dear lady to go", she confided to the school's adviser. At the end of the current year, however, the dear lady was doing just that and Miss Morgan was thankfully able to advertise for a successor.

Yet when it came to the point Miss Morgan unexpectedly had difficulty in deciding exactly what she wanted the new teacher to do — which made it difficult to write the job description. She raised it at the half-term staff meeting. Everyone knew and admired the work which Miss Brush had been doing with her remedial groups, she told them untruthfully, but it might well be difficult to find another Miss Brush, so they ought to think about the whole question of compensatory and remedial teaching in order to keep their options as wide open as possible when it came to appointing Miss Brush's successor. Did the reception class and the first year teachers, for example, think that any of their children needed extra help, and if so did they think it would be better to have this help at an earlier or a later stage?

The resulting discussion got off to a divisive start. The reception year teachers talked persuasively about the need to help some of their problem pupils and to stimulate their language development so that they could benefit from the more formal teaching in the final year. The final year teachers talked just as persuasively about the need to bring children on before they went up to the junior school when they would simply flounder if they hadn't made more progress. Gradually some concensus emerged; children might need help at any age, and they ought to expect the new teacher to accept this.

The next thing, the head told them, was to decide how the new teacher could give them most help. Several of them had mentioned how difficult they found it not to overlook individuals, or even whole groups of children in their classrooms. Others had mentioned the disruptive effect of one or two exceptional individuals. Would it be better simply to remove small groups for one or two sessions a week, or could the new teacher perhaps help them more by working alongside them in the classroom: (i) by taking over so they could concentrate on small groups, or (ii) by working with groups themselves while the teacher carried on with the majority. There had never been any team teaching at Stonerace; there were no open plan areas, but might this be an opportunity to experiment?

The teachers were divided on the idea, but it soon became plain that they were not opposed in principle. Their hesitation lay in committing themselves to working so closely with an unknown quantity who had yet to be appointed. They were less worried about his or her experience than about whether they would get on with whoever it was as a person.

The discussion ended inconclusively, but the final comments had given Miss Morgan an idea. At the beginning of the previous term she had promoted one of the younger teachers on her staff to a scale II post, giving her special responsibility for language development throughout the school. Linda Guest had tackled this enthusiastically, starting by making a list of useful materials held in the school and circulating it to all teachers with notes on the ages for which each one was suitable. She had also persuaded the Teachers' Centre to make video recordings of herself and another teacher talking with a group of children, and had used this for discussion about spoken language and comprehension with all the reception year teachers.

Miss Morgan's idea was to offer Linda an opportunity to extend her work in language and literacy by giving her 50 per cent of the week to work with other teachers in their classrooms, occasionally withdrawing groups of children to work with them herself if she saw fit. Linda would retain her responsibility as class teacher, but the new part-time teacher would also work with her class. The main advantage of this plan, Miss Morgan argued, was that Linda Guest already had the support and respect of the staff. All but one or two of them would welcome her help and would not feel threatened by her coming into their classroom.

The disadvantage lay in splitting Linda's class. She was a conscientious class teacher and thought the children might suffer from being split between two teachers. The head did not think that would matter. "If we get the right person they might even benefit from having two teachers with different skills and different ideas", she maintained. Another point she mentioned to Linda was that she thought a good applicant would welcome the chance to share a class of her own. Too often, part-time teachers spent all their time seeing groups of children for only one or two sessions a week with the result that they never got to know any of the children very well and didn't get really involved in the life of the school. With some hesitation, Linda agreed to give it a try and Miss Morgan drafted an advertisement for the authority's staffing section to insert in the educational press.

Questions

1 Can you think of examples from your own experience of schools — or teachers — which would be called "old-fashioned" by critics and "marvellous teachers — thoroughly sound" by admirers? Is either view based on anything more than prejudice?

2 Do you share Miss Morgan's doubts about Miss Brush's remedial reading groups?

3 Did Miss Brush have any educational justification in selecting only children she considered "ready" to learn to read? When is a child "ready" to learn to read?

4 What is meant by "compensatory and remedial teaching"? Are the two terms synonymous?

5 The staff meeting got off to a divisive start, with each teacher arguing her own class's needs. This sort of discussion can lead to a more constructive critical awareness of problems facing colleagues throughout the school. Alternatively it can lead to entrenched positions and bitterness when someone else gets more than her fair slice of the cake. How would you handle the meeting and subsequent discussions to ensure they were constructive?

6 As a teacher would you be happy for an experienced colleague to come into your classroom to help with backward children? What sort of tensions might this create?

7 Given the offer of help of this kind, how would you wish to organise the class to derive the maximum benefit from the arrangement?

8 Do you think Linda Guest had tackled her responsibility for language development sensibly and imaginatively? How would you tackle a similar responsibility?

9 Do you agree that the head's request to Linda Guest was the best solution to the problem caused by Miss Brush's retirement?

10 In Linda Guest's place, how would you prepare for the work you planned to do in other teachers' classes? What preliminary planning would be needed: (i) with the class teachers, (ii) with the children, and (iii) in selecting suitable activities?

Edgar

Main themes

1 Aggressive behaviour is sometimes a way of securing much-needed attention, but it can also be a necessary outlet when tension becomes too great.

2 Analysing difficult behaviour has a lot in common with assessing a child's learning difficulty.

3 Improving a child's behaviour uses the same principles as those used in remedial work; you start with something in which the child can be successful.

Edgar Royston had been placed in Helen English's class on his admission to Stonerace Infants School the previous Summer term, and she had kept the same class into their second year. Edgar was the one child who had made her regret keeping the same class. He did not have the skilful timing that could destroy a carefully-planned session in the first five minutes with a series of well-aimed questions at the teacher and well-concealed kicks at other children. A specialist in that art had caused her sleepless nights as a probationer five years earlier. Edgar was the first child to upset her seriously since that tormentor had been removed to a special school. Edgar was quite different.

He was never still; worse, he was totally unpredictable. Most of the time he would accept her instructions to sit down, stop talking, stop interfering with Jenny's work, pick up his book, pick up his pencil, stop tipping his chair backwards and forwards and so on. Occasionally, and without warning, he would leap to his feet swearing at the top of his voice and either attack her or another child with feet, fists, teeth and nails or hurl his chair at the victim of the moment. Nor were these outbursts short-lived. He could keep it up for ten or fifteen minutes, only calming down when Helen English, Miss Morgan and often another teacher had physically removed him from the classroom.

His language was fairly fruity at other times too. Recently, the parents of two other children had come to the school to complain about him. It was not fair, they said for their children to be intimidated in this way and prevented from working. Both Helen English and the head thoroughly agreed. Edgar's parents had already been invited to the school and on the third invitation they turned up. Mr Royston turned out to be a large, tough building site foreman with somewhat traditional views about child-raising and about education. "The trouble is you don't give him enough stick", he told Miss Morgan as one expert to another. "He's a little devil at home sometimes, especially with his mother, but when he gets too bad she tells me and I can tell you he doesn't do it again for a bit!"

Mrs Royston looked less certain. She was an exhausted-looking woman and the reason soon became clear. She had been married before and had one son by her previous husband. A few months after her marriage to Mr Royston, this son had been involved in a road accident and had been left paraplegic with severe brain damage and frequent attacks of *grand mal* epilepsy. Only that weekend he had had three major fits and they had needed to call an ambulance. She admitted that Edgar was less of a problem when his father was at home but hinted that he was a very different boy when his father's back was turned. He not only tormented his older stepbrother, who could do nothing to retaliate, but nagged his mother incessantly as well.

Edgar was the only child of Mrs Royston's second marriage. "Oh no, I couldn't possibly face any more", she exclaimed in horror when Helen asked if there were any other children in the family. She really did not know what approach worked with Edgar, except his father's solution of "more stick".

The interview did not seem to have helped much in deciding what to do about Edgar. Nevertheless, two good things came from it. The first was that the Roystons agreed to Edgar being seen by the school's educational psychologist if things did not improve substantially in the next few weeks. The second was that his teacher felt she understood the reasons for his behaviour more clearly.

At home Edgar was kept on a tight rein by his father. This probably wouldn't matter too much if both parents were not so pre-occupied with the care of his older stepbrother. As things were though, he felt inordinately jealous of the time and attention devoted to the vegetable-like object in a wheelchair and had to resort to fairly drastic devices to make his own presence felt. A beating from his father was obviously no fun, but Helen English supposed it might be better than being totally ignored. Alternatively, she thought, Edgar might have concluded that he could usually attract his mother's attention by being a nuisance without incurring his father's wrath, so the risk was worth taking.

Yet this analysis did not seem to explain all his behaviour in class. It explained much of the restlessness, many of the minor interruptions and the acts of interference with other children. It did not explain the sudden, unpredictable outbursts that left the whole school with jangling nerves for the rest of the day. These, she thought, must result from a gradual build-up of tension. When the pressure passed beyond a certain point the safety valve blew out — or the hand grenade exploded, depending which way you looked at it.

Edgar was referred to the local child guidance clinic a few weeks later. Eventually, the school doctor received a letter from the consultant child psychiatrist describing him as a temperamentally volatile little boy who was reacting badly to stressful family circumstances. It was not thought that individual psychotherapy would help him, and his mother had felt too busy to accept the offer of case work support from the clinic's psychiatric social worker. A note from the educational psychologist mentioned the possibility of special education in the authority's day school for maladjusted children. If the school felt this to be necessary, he would pursue the matter with the appropriate authorities. He had to point out, though, that there were unlikely to be any vacancies for another six months.

"Do you think the words 'temperamentally volatile little boy' mean that he hit the psychiatrist, or just swore at him?" Helen English asked the head as they read the report together. "You know, I'm afraid I'd like to think that he did both!" the head replied charitably, "but it looks as if we're stuck with him so we'd better try to think of something ourselves."

Since the beginning of the year Linda Guest had been spending half a session in Helen English's class twice a week. Inevitably, she found herself spending rather less time on language and literacy work and rather more time with Edgar than she had originally intended. It seemed logical therefore to bring her into the discussion about Edgar's management.

They decided quickly that no straightforward approach such as ignoring bad behaviour and giving him praise for good behaviour would be effective. Edgar's disruption was of a kind that could not be ignored. Whatever the text books might say, he would soon have the whole class in pandemonium. Yet there were things which he did like doing: he liked working with Linda; he liked helping Helen English tidy up at the end of the lesson and prepare books and equipment for the next lesson; he liked collecting the empty milk bottles and helping to take them to the yard for collection. There were also things he did not like: he did not like being made to sit at a desk on his own, nor did he like having to sit on a chair outside Miss Morgan's study.

Helen English and Linda Guest reckoned that they could cope with most of Edgar's behaviour if they used these likes and dislikes systematically enough. The question was to know where to begin. It would be hopeless expecting Edgar to behave like any other child before allowing him to do one of the things he regarded as a privilege. Similarly, if they made him sit on his own for five minutes every time he did anything wrong he would spend the whole lesson on his own.

They decided to start in a small way. For a week they would make him sit on a chair outside the classroom for five minutes every time he hit, bumped into, pushed, or in any way physically interfered with another child. He would not be punished in this way for any other sort of behaviour, however objectionable. At the end of every session he got through without being sent outside he would be allowed to choose from a list of privileges which she and Helen English had jointly prepared. If he was not sent out at all between Linda Guest's two sessions with the class, she would spend fifteen minutes working or playing with him on his own in the little classroom set aside for group work.

The first fortnight saw reasonable progress. Edgar was made to sit on the chair outside the classroom three times, but these had all been in the first week, and they decided to include swearing and abusive language in the programme. For the first week all went well; it was the most peaceful week Helen English remembered since she had started teaching Edgar. He was responding well to her attention at the end of each session, and eagerly looked forward to his time with Miss Guest. At the beginning of the second week he came to school in a bad temper on Monday morning; things got progressively worse as the day progressed, culminating in a temper tantrum to end all temper tantrums, an hour before the end of afternoon school. After an exhausting half-hour the wind seemed to go out of his sails, he burst into tears and refused to talk to anyone.

Edgar normally walked home, but this time the head sent a message to his mother to come and collect him. She arrived in a hurry and in a temper. She and her husband had had enough of Edgar. The stepbrother had been worse than usual over the weekend, but all Edgar could do was get in his parents' way, and poke, hit or kick the invalid. He had been given two hidings, and after the second one in the middle of Sunday lunch had been sent to bed for the rest of the day without any tea or supper. In the morning he had started again, and had stormed out of the house without any breakfast. "So lunchtime today was his first food for 24 hours", exclaimed Miss Morgan. "I don't know, and I don't care", snapped Mrs Royston.

Questions

1 Edgar's behaviour seemed totally unpredictable at first. Was it in fact unpredictable in the light of the information obtained from his parents? What aspects of his home circumstances make his behaviour less hard to understand?

2 What is *grand mal* epilepsy? What action should a teacher take if a child has an attack at school?

3 What lessons do you think Edgar learnt from his father's and mother's approaches to discipline at home?

4 Do you agree with Helen English's assessment of the reasons for Edgar's behaviour in class?

5 Referral to the child guidance clinic did not turn out to be of much practical help to Edgar's teachers. How might members of the clinic team have offered something more useful?

6 Is there evidence that the clinic team saw themselves as experts offering diagnoses and – in approved cases – treatment? Is there room for a different model in which outside agencies see themselves as equal partners working with teachers to solve – or at least reduce – problems?

7 When is it possible to ignore bad behaviour? Is this likely to be successful without the teacher making a point of noticing those things the child does well and praising him for them?

8 Helen English and Linda Guest based their programme for Edgar on careful observation of his likes and dislikes. How is this similar to the assessment of a child's difficulty with reading?

9 Comment on the programme for Edgar's management.

10 Describe Edgar's behaviour and his teachers' programme to modify it in terms of reinforcement principles.

11 Was any possible physical basis to Edgar's bad temper on Monday morning suggested by the information his mother provided?

12 Edgar's life at home seems to be becoming intolerable both for him and for his family. To whom might the head refer the family for further help?

13 What arguments can you think of for taking Edgar into the care of the local authority? What are the arguments against this course of action?

PART III
Secondary schools and their pupils

Bridge End Comprehensive

Main themes

1 A high quality of remedial teaching in a special class is no substitute for flexible provision throughout the school.

2 If remedial teaching aims to remedy, then its content must reflect the curriculum in the rest of the school.

Miss Brown supposed that they would have to do something − "To keep them quiet at the office", she explained in a slightly resigned way to her deputy and assistant head at their weekly meeting. The school's remedial department had been the subject of a politely acrimonious discussion the previous day, when the authority's senior adviser for remedial education had made one of her infrequent visits to inform Miss Brown that complaints had been received from three parents.

The adviser had referred all three children to "child guidance" − a term she still insisted on using in spite of the fact that the former child guidance system had been replaced years earlier by a hospital-based department of child psychiatry and the l.e.a.'s own psychological service. In this case there was no doubt that she meant the educational psychologist when she said child guidance, since the psychologist had visited Bridge End a week earlier. "He came, he saw and he went", snapped Miss Brown, "and then he persuaded them at the office that we, like Gaul, are divided into three parts!"

"Well I suppose it's true, though he might have avoided the classical allusion", said the deputy peaceably. "We have got two ability-based bands, subdivided into sets for most subjects, and the remedial department is a third ability band, however you look at it". "Yes, I know, but at the moment we're not discussing either of our prejudices about mixed-ability teaching". Miss Brown had always doubted the wisdom of her decision to bow to pressure from colleagues, the office and a minority of parents, in abandoning clear-cut − her opponents called it rigid − streaming in favour of the present banding system. On the other hand, she also prided herself on the provision the school made for its least able pupils. This, she firmly believed was one of the things comprehensive schools were all about.

Indeed, the provision was quite impressive. Diana Thorne's remedial department contained three other full-time teachers, who between them catered for about twenty children from each of the school's four main year groups. They shared the teaching of each class between them, providing what was in effect a school within a school. Attendance of pupils in the remedial department tended to be better than that of the less able pupils in the lower of the two larger ability bands. Most of the staff were happy about the arrangement; all the teachers in the remedial department were happy with it, and had already made clear that they saw no need for a looser structure to integrate them more closely into the work of the rest of the school.

There were only three clouds on this happy horizon. The first, as the educational psychologist had politely pointed out to Miss Brown, and more forcefully to the remedial adviser, was that no child in the remedial department had apparently yet aspired to the dizzy heights of CSE Mode 3 in any science subject, and there were a number of other respects in which the syllabus was deficient, for example, inadequate PE facilities for the boys. This had in fact been the substance of one of the complaints to the office. The second, was that transfer in and out of the remedial department was unusual and difficult to arrange, precisely because of the self-sufficient nature of the department. Miss Brown had always recognised this, but still couldn't help feeling irritated when the adviser had asked her how many children had moved out of the remedial department in each of the last three years. (The answer was two, none and one). The third, was the related fact that children with specific learning difficulties in the mainstream of the school had no opportunity to receive special help. This was the cause of the other two complaints to the office, "Although to be fair it sounds as if these parents were asking where they could get help outside the school rather than complaining about us", said Miss Brown.

"So the question is how we tackle it", remarked the assistant head. "There's a *prima-facie* case that we've been falling down, so we ought to involve the staff in a study of the needs of children with problems, both in and out of the remedial department. We've obviously got to involve Diana Thorne", she continued, "but in such a way that she doesn't dig her heels in and just looks for arguments against changing the *status quo*. Another obvious person to involve is Roy Dane – he's the senior year tutor and he knows more about children with problems, both academic and personal, than anyone else. The trouble is that he and Diana haven't always seen eye to eye, but I think it's about time they were made to recognise each other's qualities. What do you feel about telling them they are forming a working party, with me as chairman, to report to you on the achievements of the remedial department and the additional needs of children in the rest of the school?"

"Thank you, that should lead to a lovely relationship", replied Miss Brown, thinking of the two incidents when she had needed to intervene personally to prevent disagreements between Diana Thorne and Roy Dane from souring staff room relationships. "I think that if it's going to work we've got to get them thinking about fairly specific questions. You might draw up guidelines and let me see them next week".

The assistant head's guidelines were short and to the point:

(*i*) How many pupils in bands 1 and 2 need special help with one or more of the basic skills, reading, writing and maths, which cannot easily be provided in the course of their ordinary lessons?

(*ii*) How many children in the remedial department could cope with the curriculum and activities of band 2?

(*iii*) How much overlap is there between the attainments of the top children in the remedial department and the bottom of band 2, and how far is this reflected in common curriculum?

"That third question", said Miss Brown "will hoist Diana by her own petard – she's always telling people about the marvellous progress of children in her department. I'll have a word with her and with Roy this lunchtime, and then it'll be up to the three of you".

The working party made erratic progress. To their credit, both Diana Thorne and Roy Dane buried their differences and accepted their terms of reference with only the smallest murmur. Two problems emerged fairly quickly. It was all very well asking teachers which children needed special help that could not be provided in the normal class. The difficulty lay in persuading them: (i) that if they admitted that such children did exist this would not be seen as a reflection on their own ability, and (ii) that the children would not forthwith be removed to the remedial department "for full-time incarceration, I mean treatment", the head of biology explained to Roy Dane.

A more typical comment was elicited when Roy asked an English teacher about a child's handwriting. The question was prompted by the boy's English report the previous term: "A likeable boy who tries very hard and given time can achieve good results; he is handicapped by his slow and poor handwriting; very fluent orally". The reply to Roy's inquiry was, "Well, yes, his handwriting is appallingly slow; he might well be capable of GCE "O" level if it wasn't for this – but there's absolutely no way, Roy, that you'll get me to say he's remedial!"

The second problem was that the remedial teachers tended "to play it by ear". This left them infinite scope for developing project work arising from the pupils' interests, but meant that their curriculum records were scanty to say the least. They monitored the children's progress in reading and maths with a series of tests that sounded impressive until the head of maths remarked that they were based on ideas of maths teaching that he and his department had abandoned as antiquated eight years earlier. The real problem, though, was that the remedial teachers could not say which children could cope with some ordinary lessons, as they did not know enough about the curriculum and methods in the rest of the school.

Predictably, getting over this problem depended almost entirely on the degree of co-operation between Diana Thorne and the subject teachers in the rest of the school. The heads of the maths, science and social studies departments all indicated a willingness to sit down with the working party and look at the possibility of some of the remedial children returning to "ordinary" lessons.

The head of the English department passed the matter on to a probationer and returned to his "A" level teaching.

Gradually a satisfactory level of agreement was reached. The working party agreed, to no one's surprise, that more or less full-time provision would continue to be needed for some children. Diana Thorne accepted, however, that there could be no real harm in a trial which involved all remedial pupils joining the other classes in band 2 for PE, music and art. She was a little more surprised to find herself agreeing that the children who needed more or less full-time remedial provision were not always the slowest or dullest in the school. Often they were just the more difficult ones who were temperamentally unstable or under stress at home, and needed a smaller class with fewer demands. "I've never been happy about calling them remedial", she said untruthfully, adding — more accurately — "but I think we can do more for them than anyone else in the school at the moment".

It was also agreed, with considerably more difficulty, that a small number of children were experiencing severe difficulties in ordinary lessons who might benefit from part-time help from the remedial teachers on a withdrawal group basis. "I'll give it a try and we'll see if you can do anything for James' handwriting", said the head of English to Diana and the assistant head, "but I warn you that if it doesn't work I'll fight you tooth and nail to get him back!" "Lovely to have friends", Diana murmured when he returned to his office.

The working party's report to Miss Brown was studiously low key. It proposed the following:

(*i*) that the staffing of the remedial department should remain unaltered;

(*ii*) that the number of full-time remedial pupils admitted in the next school year should be twelve to fifteen rather than twenty;

(*iii*) that all the full-time remedial pupils should be integrated with band 2 for PE, art and music;

(*iv*) that there should be continuing discussions between the head of the remedial department and the heads of all subject departments with the aim of facilitating movement in and out of the remedial department on a full-time or part-time basis;

(*v*) that the department should establish a number of withdrawal groups for children with exceptional difficulties in the mainstream of the school.

Miss Brown approved the report and put it on the agenda of the next staff meeting for probable implementation in the next school year. Correctly, she thought it would not impress the l.e.a.'s remedial adviser, who would object to the complacent acceptance of difficult children being regarded as dull, and would want a more explicit, and far more literal, interpretation of the aims of *remedial* teaching. In the circumstances of Bridge End Comprehensive, however, Miss Brown thought the document a constructive and sensible step forward.

Questions

1 How does a Child Guidance Clinic differ from the network of hospital-based and l.e.a.-based services described here?

2 What are the strengths and limitations of each system from the differing viewpoints of schools and of children or parents?

3 Would it be fair to describe the system of ability bands subdivided into sets as "sophisticated streaming"?

4 Is segregation of the brightest and dullest pupils in the school consistent with a policy of non-selective intake?

5 Do you agree that provision in the remedial department was "quite impressive"?

6 How would you expect science to be covered in a full-time remedial department of the sort described at Bridge End?

7 Is there a valid case for a remedial department to cater for its pupils full-time with little movement in or out?

8 What is meant by the term "specific learning difficulty"? Give examples of children in your own ordinary classes who might have some form of specific learning difficulty. What are the implications: (*i*) for your own teaching, (*ii*) for the child himself, and (*iii*) for the school's policy on remedial teaching?

9 What are your views on the assistant head's guidelines? Is he right to assume that some children have difficulties which cannot easily be provided for in the course of their ordinary lessons?

10 Do you think the working party might have had a greater chance of success if it had included some heads of department?

11 Explain in detail how the remedial department could have improved its record keeping.

12 The head of maths regarded the remedial department's tests as out of date. What are the other limitations of traditional attainment tests?

13 Is it right, in a comprehensive school, that more or less full-time remedial provision should be needed for some children? What are the dangers inherent in this attitude?

14 Is there any educational justification for children being placed in the remedial department because of their difficult behaviour? What does this imply about the school's "hidden curriculum"?

15 What do you regard as the strengths and limitations of the working party's recommendations?

Robert

Main themes
1 Educational isolation in an internally well-run remedial department can lead to social isolation in "the thick class".
2 This can affect the child's adjustment at home.

3 Latent tensions at home can be triggered off by problems at school.

Robert Peterson was not one of the three pupils whose parents had complained to the office about the provision of remedial teaching at Bridge End School. Twelve years old, he was in his second term at the school and had been placed in the remedial department on the basis of a reading test carried out by Diana Thorne on her visit to his primary school the term before he was due to start at Bridge End. His reading age was in fact "borderline" for the department at 8.5, but he was said to be a bit shy and uncertain of himself and to need a small class.

As she talked to his parents, Miss Brown wondered privately if the school was not catering rather well for Robert. He had always been shy, had always had difficulty with his reading, had always tended to lack confidence in himself. He sounded altogether an ideal child for Diana Thorne's department.

But it wasn't as simple as that, his mother explained patiently. It wasn't even as simple as the fact that he was in the "thick class" and felt acutely upset about this, although it had taken her hours to discover the fact. "I know Miss Thorne does an awful lot for them, and it's not her or the teaching I'm worried about", Mrs Peterson explained hastily. "It's just that the other children call it the thick class and his younger brother's got hold of it now as well."

Mrs Peterson was not in fact complaining about Robert being placed in the remedial department, which made a change, Miss Brown thought to herself. The things she was worried about were that his stammer had returned after four years without it, that he seemed tense and unhappy most of the time, except during school holidays, that his interest and ability in maths seemed to be declining, and that he was not joining in any out-of-school activities because he felt too unsure of himself.

Miss Brown liked the Petersons; they seemed caring parents, anxious for advice, not out to make a fuss. She thanked them for calling, said she would make full inquiries and telephone them again before the end of the week to discuss what the school could do or suggest that might help Robert.

The problem was passed to Robert's year tutor, Roy Dane. "Well, you'll obviously have to discuss this one with Diana; what with the working party and now this, you two really are getting together!" remarked an assistant year tutor cheerfully.

Robert's educational record card contained little useful information apart from the fact that his arithmetic grade had always been B or C on an A−E scale, throughout his primary school years. Indeed there didn't appear to have been any educational problem apart from the difficulty with reading. Even this had apparently not been considered serious enough to warrant referral to the educational psychologist. The school medical officer was quite helpful. Robert had a history of stammering, but this had cleared up in the course of treatment with the speech therapy service by the time he was eight. There was a brief report saying that his stammer was caused by tension, but nothing about the reason for the tension. Apart from the stammer he had always been a physically fit boy, said the doctor.

Diana was surprisingly defensive about Robert's progress. She thought his maths was "all right" but showed Roy the sort of book he could read without difficulty and explained the remedial reading work she and another teacher were doing with him. She also pointed out how withdrawn he was; did Roy really think a child like this could cope in band 2? Roy, however, was not convinced. He recognised that Robert needed help to acquire greater confidence and greater fluency in reading, and to improve his comprehension of what he read. At the moment he was concentrating so hard on reading each word correctly that he seemed to have no energy left to concentrate on the meaning. But this alone did not justify full-time placement in the remedial department.

Diana made it clear that in her view the problem lay at home. The parents must be putting too much pressure on him to do well at school, not giving him a chance to establish himself in his new school. Her view was based on a discussion with the primary school head teacher, and two brief meetings with the Petersons on open evenings.

Robert himself was difficult to interview, both because of his stammer and because of his shyness. Yes, he liked Miss Thorne, and his other teachers; he liked some of the other pupils in his class; there was no one outside his class he really disliked. When asked if he was teased or bullied at all, his stammer became worse, but Roy Dane was rather bewildered to find that although Robert said this did happen, it was not at school, nor was it from friends he played with at home.

Eventually Roy dropped the subject and asked if Robert had ever thought of joining any of the lunchtime or after-school clubs. After a very long pause Robert said no, but on further questioning he admitted that he had enjoyed drama at his primary school, and liked swimming. It appeared that he had not asked to join in these activities because he did not know the teachers who organised them. This, Roy realised, was solely because Robert was in the remedial department, since both the teachers concerned taught all the first year children for at least one lesson a week.

Roy wondered how to follow up Diana's belief that Robert's behaviour at school was caused by tensions at home. One possibility was to refer the matter to the education welfare officer, or even the educational psychologist, but without more to go on he did not feel justified in doing this. Instead, with the head's approval, he telephoned Mrs Peterson and explained that he had been making inquiries and thought they would be able to take steps to help Robert settle more happily in the school. He didn't like to ask them to come to school yet again, unless they preferred to come rather than discuss it over the telephone. As he had hoped, the Petersons wanted to come.

He explained that he had spoken to the teachers who took the out-of-school swimming and drama groups; both would be happy for Robert to join the groups and he would tell Robert when to go to ask them. Both parents saw the sense of Robert making the approach himself. He had also, with some difficulty, arranged for Robert to join a maths set in the higher range of the second ability band and at the start of the next school year he would be with the mainstream for certain other lessons too. Meanwhile, Miss Thorne would explain to the Petersons and Robert together the purpose and aims of the remedial reading programme which she had drawn up for Robert.

Finally, there was one thing on which he wondered if the Petersons could help him. Roy Dane explained Robert's reluctance to say who was teasing him. "Good lord, that's Tracy", exclaimed both parents. Robert, it appeared, got on well with his brother but not with his sister. She imitated his stammer and teased him for being in the "thick class". "Robert gets mad at her, but that just makes her worse; we try to stop her, but I don't know what she likes more, us trying to stop her or him getting mad!"

The Petersons seemed to accept this friction as a normal, passing phase in family life. They also seemed happy with the outcome of the visit. Roy Dane suggested that if they were still unhappy about Robert's adjustment at school after another month or so, they should get in touch with him again. They could also let him know if things did not get better at home, and he would try to think of someone who might be able to help relieve the tension.

Questions

1 Would you expect a reading age of 8.5 to be "border-line" for the remedial department?

2 What does Mrs Peterson's interview with the head tell you about her attitude towards the school?

3 What does "the thick class" stigma tell you about the school? How could the school reduce this negative labelling?

4 Was it desirable that the Petersons should see the head on their first visit? Who else might they have seen?

5 What investigations would you make — or request — if a child's stammer recurred after four years?

6 Is Diana Thorne right to think a withdrawn child should not be exposed to the larger classes and less protected environment of band 2?

7 Discuss some of the unstated reasons why Diana Thorne might have felt that the problem lay at home.

8 In Roy Dane's position, would you have pursued the question of bullying with Robert?

9 Robert had not met two teachers because he was in the school's remedial department. What are the ways this sort of problem could be overcome?

10 Do you think Roy Dane was right not to refer the problem to an outside agency?

11 How do the Petersons make the problem worse at home?

12 Draw up a detailed programme to help the Petersons improve relationships between Robert and his sister.

Blacksmith Lane Comprehensive

Main themes

1 Opening a unit or appointing a counsellor can be seen as a palliative, tackling the symptoms without doing anything about the cause.

2 Developing a policy of mixed-ability teaching requires support for staff in the area of classroom management as well as in-service training in the organisation and presentation of the curriculum.

"I'm sorry Derek, but I can't see any point at all either in appointing a counsellor or in setting up a unit; and I still wouldn't see any point even if I thought the authority would give us staff and money to do it." Vick Watkin leant back wearily. He liked Derek Turner, his deputy head with overall responsibility for pastoral care, liaison with outside agencies and discipline, but he couldn't always see the wood for the trees.

The trouble was, thought Vick, that Derek saw all the children referred by staff for disruptive behaviour, and he quite rightly wanted to do some thing more constructive than caning them. "Mind you, with the number standing outside my door each lunchtime and at the end of the afternoon, I might benefit from the exercise if I did cane them all!" said Derek, thoughtfully stroking his ample belly. "But seriously, if we're not going to appoint a counsellor or open a unit, we've got to think of something, if only for the morale of the staff. They're complaining like hell as it is."

Here the head entirely agreed with his deputy; he had himself noticed the strain on the staff in the last two terms. It was his third year in the school, and the most testing one so far. The first had been peaceful enough while he found his feet, and senior, experienced staff who had been at the school as long as the previous head continued to operate the well-oiled machinery. In the course of his second year he had instituted a few small changes, mainly involving the option system for the fourth and fifth years, but the main emphasis had been on preparation for a major re-organisation at the start of his third year. This involved a switch from three ability bands, with setting within each band in English, French, maths and science, to a mixed-ability system with setting only in maths. True, the switch applied only to the first two year groups, but it was planned to extend it each year, so that in three years' time the whole school would operate a mixed-ability system.

Although only the first two years were mixed ability at the moment, the strain was showing. Vick Watkin had gone into it with his eyes open; both he and the school's general adviser were all too well aware of the distinction between mixed-ability teaching and formal teaching in a class of mixed-ability children. He had been fortunate in appointing new heads of the English, French and science faculties shortly after he took up his post. The head of social studies had reluctantly agreed to fall into line, but the head of the maths department had insisted there was no way he could possibly agree to abandon setting.

The problem was that although most of the faculty heads supported the change, the same did not apply to all the heads of department within each faculty, and many other teachers had regarded the changes with apprehension. They were now seeing their worst fears realised as they struggled to maintain the same standards of work and discipline as they had been used to in settled classes. The first year children fresh from primary schools, were settling better than the second year which had found their feet in the old banded system. To make matters worse, the additional clerical support which Vick Watkin regarded as essential to successful mixed-ability teaching, had not materialised in spite of the authority's promises.

There were two further problems. First, Blacksmith Lane School had had an influx of probationers in each of the last two years. These inexperienced teachers were now struggling to cope with the challenge of mixed-ability teaching without adequate support from more senior staff, who felt under pressure themselves. The second problem was that as deputy, Derek Turner headed a team of five year tutors, and in Vick Watkin's opinion at least two of these year tutors should never have been given responsibility for pastoral care, let alone counselling.

Both believed in theory that their job was to try to find out what was troubling children, not to act as disciplinarians in support of colleagues. This might have been acceptable, (though Vick Watkin would have had reservations) had they been consistent. What happened in fact was that they occasionally panicked, either because of the number of children sent to them by subject teachers or because patient talking was getting nowhere. When this happened they became old-fashioned disciplinarians and wielded the cane. As a result, neither teachers nor children knew what to expect.

The picture was not entirely black. A number of the teachers who had supported the mixed-ability policy were already noticing a change for the better in classroom discipline and general relationships between teachers and pupils. Vick Watkin knew from his previous experience that this trend would continue as the staff became more confident in mixed-ability teaching. Nevertheless, at present the satisfied teachers were in a minority and if he was not careful he might find himself facing a crisis of disruptive behaviour from certain pupils (or certain classes, he thought, privately) and a crisis of confidence from his staff.

Yet the fact remained that the problems were being created by the system. Blacksmith Lane had a disproportionate number of probationers, inconsistent practice in discipline and pastoral care which resulted in uncertainty and insecurity for teachers and children alike, and a new teaching policy for which the staff were receiving inadequate support.

In principle, Vick Watkin thought, a unit for disruptive pupils, or even a school counsellor might be able to relieve pressure on certain teachers, giving them time to find their feet and to re-adjust. He was quite certain, though, that no school with a well-balanced and well-taught curriculum, and satisfactory pastoral care organisation, should need this sort of palliative. He had taught in large, inner-city schools before coming to Blacksmith Lane, and if they didn't need units there was no earthly reason why Blacksmith Lane should.

The weakness, he concluded reluctantly, lay partly in the preparation for mixed-ability teaching, but more in the lack of continuing in-service training and support now that the change had been made. The theory had been well covered in courses laid on by the authority's advisers, and the faculty heads provided a high quality of help and advice in planning work to cover a wide ability range, the use of work cards, and so on. The weakness lay in help and advice with coping with the practical problems of classroom control while trying to master a new approach.

Vick's analysis was accepted by his two deputy heads, but neither saw that the analysis took them much further forward. They also accepted the limitations of a unit and recognised that, in any case, no additional provision could be made available until the start of the next school year. "What I think we need", Vick Watkin continued, "is a new post for a senior teacher, probably on scale IV, with minimal teaching responsibilities. We need someone with successful experience of mixed-ability teaching and a commitment to it, who is also experienced in dealing with disruptive behaviour. I think it's just possible that I might persuade the authority to grant us a couple of extra points; we are one of the few secondary schools which is not over-staffed. If so, we could add two points of our own to make a scale IV."

Derek Turner and the other deputy were sceptical. Even if the authority was willing to help, they were not certain how the proposed new teacher would fit into the existing staff structure. What, for example, would be his role *vis à vis* heads of departments and the heads of faculties? And how would he fit into the pastoral care system? Vick Watkin was undismayed. The pastoral care system was in need of review anyway, but he thought it should continue to investigate and take action on cases of individual children. The new teacher's job would be to work with the teachers who referred these children. They all agreed that many of the problems were arising in the first place because of problems in teaching organisation and methods, so the classroom was the place to start tackling them.

Regarding the heads of faculties, Vick Watkin thought the new appointee should have overall responsibility for probationer teachers and for co-ordinating in-service education within the school. This would continue to be needed as the mixed-ability policy extended upwards, and the courses at the l.e.a.'s Teachers' Centre were too remote for most of the staff. "I can see that it might work", said Derek Turner thoughtfully, "but it'll depend on the sort of person you get, more than any other post I can think of — except perhaps yours", he added more cheerfully, looking at Vick.

Questions

1 What are the advantages and the dangers of mixed-ability teaching?

2 What non-teaching support is needed if mixed-ability teaching is to be successful?

3 What is meant by the distinction between mixed-ability teaching and formal teaching in a class of mixed-ability children?

4 What administrative difficulties might be created by the gradual introduction of mixed-ability teaching, starting with the first year?

5 The maths department was the only one which could not see its way clear to abandoning setting. Does this reflect the nature of the subject, or simply the way it is normally taught in school? Can the concept of "maths across the curriculum" overcome the traditional problems which arise in teaching this subject?

6 The head did not accept the year tutors' distinction between: (i) finding out what was troubling children, and (ii) acting as disciplinarians in support of colleagues. Do you?

7 How could the head have clarified the year tutors' responsibilities to help them avoid the inconsistent sort of reaction described?

8 Do you accept the head's view that if the large, inner-city schools at which he had previously taught did not need units, then there was no reason why Blacksmith Lane should?

9 Can you see flaws in the head's analysis of the school's present problems?

10 What are the possible advantages and dangers in his proposed solution? Write a job description that would recognise the dangers and imply possible ways to overcome them.

Annie

Main themes

1 Motivating a child who has made up her mind that she cannot make educational progress requires sympathetic but active co-operation between teachers and parents, in which each sees the others as partners.

2 Motivating teachers to try once more with a child who has so far defied all their efforts, requires active and practical help and support from the advisory services.

Annie was not the sort of girl Vick Watkin had had in mind when he persuaded the local education authority to support him in appointing Chris Pemberton to a scale IV post with responsibility for the integration of slow learning and disturbed pupils into the school's mixed-ability classes. Chris's appointment was based on the belief that if the curriculum and the methods of teaching it are right, problems arising from deprived or disturbed homes could be sorted out on their own merits, without being confused with problems caused or aggravated by school limitations.

Annie, however, was a test for any system. A large West Indian thirteen-year-old, she never missed a day's schooling, and never did an hour's work while she was there. It was not a case of her being dull and unable to cope with the work. She had been referred to the educational psychologist by her primary school but he had merely confirmed their own suspicions; whatever the reason for her lack of progress, she was not dull. He had, in fact, given her an IQ test – rather furtively, as in public he professed the belief that these tests were totally inappropriate for West Indian children. Inappropriate or not, Annie had a verbal scale IQ of 110, on the Wechsler Intelligence Scale for Children, and a performance (abstract reasoning) scale IQ of 115.

On arrival at Blacksmith Lane she read as well as the average eight-year-old and appeared to have given up all hope of making progress. Given a reading book appropriate to her reading age she would say, quite truthfully, "That's kids' stuff". If she was persuaded to persist she would do so, while making it completely clear that she was only co-operating to humour the teacher. In most lessons she simply sat at the back of the class and either went to sleep or annoyed her neighbours. If pressed to do some work it was a case of, "I can't read, Miss!"

Annie had a temper. She only lost it occasionally, but when she did the effect was quite dramatic. "When pushed too far", her primary school report had read, "she flies off the handle, swearing, shouting and throwing things about". Annie had never actually assaulted a teacher but the three outbursts in her twelve months at Blacksmith Lane had caused a stir all round the school.

She was in her second year when Chris Pemberton joined the staff. She had already been placed in classes with only the most experienced teachers. They, however, treated her with kid gloves and went out of their way to avoid confrontation – which in Annie's case meant avoiding anything she thought she might find difficult – which meant more or less everything that her class did.

Annie was an obvious case for Chris to look at. "Bit unfair to give you one like this to start with really", said Derek Turner sorrowfully, "but her teachers really do need help, and no one elso has a clue what to do with her!" Chris did not doubt for a moment that Annie's teachers *needed* help, but comments he had already overheard in the staff room made him doubt very much whether they *wanted* it. "I can see that your heart bleeds for me", he told Derek. "I appreciate that!"

To start with, he reviewed all the reports on Annie. Her school career had been chequered, with several changes of primary school and a total of at least a year lost through illness in her junior school. Now, however, she appeared in excellent health. Her parents seldom turned up at open evenings, but everyone who had visited the home found them welcoming and co-operative, though disappointed by Annie's obvious lack of progress.

There was one thing, though, which Chris doubted. "When pushed too far", the primary school head had written, "she flies off the handle". The descriptions Chris had heard of her outbursts at Blacksmith Lane did not quite tally with this. To start with, each tantrum had occurred with young teachers who were most unlikely to have pushed her too far. One was a student and the others a male and a female probationer, both of whom erred on the side of not pushing children hard enough rather than the reverse. All three had been extremely upset by the incidents, blaming their own inexperience. A second point was that Annie had never actually hurt anyone in a temper, either at Blacksmith Lane or at her primary schools. Now this seemed odd to Chris. She was a strong girl and if she was genuinely as hysterically out of control as the reports claimed, she would surely have left her mark on someone by now. Could Annie be an exceptionally good actor, he wondered, who used her reputation for temper to intimidate teachers into leaving her alone, making no demands on her?

Annie's parents had been to the school on two previous occasions, both arising from her outbursts. They had expressed amazement, insisting that she never did this at home. No one had ever sat down with them to discuss her dismal educational progress since the educational psychologist had pronounced – to their intense relief – that she was not ESN(M).

Chris decided it was time to involve Annie's parents more directly in her education. With Derek Turner's permission, he also asked the psychologist to re-open his file on Annie. There were three problems: (i) how to bring pressure on the parents to bring pressure on Annie to – as Chris indelicately put it – pull out her finger and start learning; (*ii*) how to provide Annie with work appropriate to her age and ability in her mixed-ability class; (*iii*) what pressure to advise Annie's teachers to bring on her if she didn't co-operate.

The psychologist was more helpful than Chris had dared to expect. She had already assessed Annie's reading retardation in detail and had been able to discover no cognitive or perceptual explanations. "Frankly I agree with you that this girl's getting away with murder", she said. "I guess it started with her frequent changes of school between the ages of five and nine, followed by her two years of intermittent illness. I think now, that she's just made up her mind that she can't read and she uses her temper to dissuade anyone from making her risk failure by trying. She's got it all worked out nicely!"

There was one possibility, though. Annie was certainly not ESN(M) in the generally accepted sense. Normally children would not go to this sort of special school with an IQ above 75 or so. On the other hand, the administrative definition in the Statutory Instrument following the 1944 Education Act made clear that the category could also cover educationally retarded children — which obviously included Annie. "Her parents won't like that at all", remarked Chris Pemberton. "You know how sensitive the West Indian community is to its children being dumped in special schools".

The psychologist replied carefully, "Yes, and they are quite right to be. Both educational psychologists, school doctors and teachers have a shabby record in that respect. What's more, I'm not going to recommend Annie for a special school. What I can do, though, is tell her parents that you are obviously right in thinking she is making no progress here. And I can say that if you claim that you can't offer her the sort of teaching she needs, the only other school the Chief Education Officer could possibly provide would be a special school. I'd only be willing to tell them that, though, if you satisfied me that you had done everything possible to help her".

"Which is where I come in", said Chris dryly. "I've talked to each of her teachers in the last fortnight, and I've got a copy of their syllabus, lesson by lesson for the next six weeks. It took some getting in one or two cases, but one head of department thanked me for succeeding where he had failed — getting one of his colleagues to plan ahead. Now I'd like you", he turned to the psychologist, "to arrange for an advisory teacher to help me prepare work cards, suitable for a child with a reading age of seven, relevant to the content of each lesson. Then I'll give them to each teacher, who will return them to me at the end of each day. I will be seeing Annie twice a day myself, to review any problems that arise."

"In addition", he continued, "I shall be giving Annie her work cards to take home to her parents each day with a note from me about her work and behaviour. They will sign the note as proof that they have seen it and Annie will return it and the cards to me next day. I'm also going to ask all teachers to sit Annie at the front of the class and to insist on her taking part in oral work as well as completing her work cards. After one month we shall review the situation internally and where necessary prepare further work cards when the first six weeks' supply runs out. I hope, though, that some teachers will feel able to produce their own by then. Naturally, we will also see Annie herself and her parents again too."

After some more discussion the meeting broke up and Chris arranged for Annie's parents to meet him and the psychologist later that week. They were overjoyed at his plan. "No one's ever tried to help like this before", they exclaimed. It seemed a pity to introduce a note of threat, but the psychologist felt she had to explain the reasons why they were asking for the Lewis' help in this final attempt to motivate their daughter. "I am sure she is capable of doing well here", she told them, "and I'm sure that if you and Annie's teachers work together she will make progress. But if she doesn't, it's only fair to tell you now that the Chief Education Officer will almost certainly have to consider moving her to a special school." Both parents were alarmed. "She will, just you wait, she will get on", they said firmly.

Questions

1 Why did the educational psychologist consider IQ tests totally inappropriate for West Indian children?

2 Are IQ tests really necessary for *any* children if the teachers' record-keeping and monitoring of progress are adequate?

3 How do you get over the problem that a thirteen-year-old, retarded in reading, regards books with a suitable reading level as "kids' stuff"? What books are available with a low reading age and a high interest age?

4 To what extent is it right to treat children "with kid gloves" to avoid confrontation?

5 Can you think of children you have taught who occasionally "fly off the handle", yet always seem to avoid hurting themselves or other people? What does Annie learn from teachers' and pupils' reactions to her temper?

6 What would you do about Annie's temper tantrums, immediately after one occurred and in the long run?

7 Do you agree with the psychologist that Annie was "getting away with murder"? Can you think of children you have taught who achieve the same sort of success?

8 What other form of special school might possibly be considered for Annie?

9 What do you think of the ethics of the educational psychologist's proposal? What do you think of the way Chris Pemberton used the psychologist?

10 Can you fault Christ Pemberton's programme for Annie's remedial treatment?

11 Could Chris Pemberton's programme reasonably be regarded as pastoral care? Does pastoral care include active support for — and advice to — class teachers?

12 Do you think the sort of support Chris Pemberton was offering teachers and Annie provides the basis for a successful alternative to a behavioural unit or a full-time counsellor?

Southlands Secondary School

Main themes

1 A school's "pastoral care" system should include support for staff as well as for children.

2 The use of corporal punishment often reflects weaknesses and/or tensions in the staff.

3 Corporal punishment can create more problems than it solves.

Tom Snelgrove's six-year-old grandson was an irrepressible extrovert with a six-year-old's ruthlessly accurate perception of mood. He was also used to doing and saying more or less as he liked on his fortnightly visits to his grandpa. In fact the behaviour which was good-humouredly tolerated would have astonished both teachers and pupils at Southlands Secondary School where grandpa was undisputed king of his educational castle. This time, however, the little boy was getting too close to the bone for comfort.

"Grandpa is angry; Grandpa is very angry; Grandpa is extremely angry; Grandpa is fantastically, extraordinarily, tremendously angry!" he chanted. Grandpa's nerve suddenly snapped, "Shut up, or I'll burn every Mister Men book you've got!" he roared.

Had he known the reason for his grandfather's anger, the little boy might not have tempted his luck. Corporal punishment had never been much of an issue at the school. The staff accepted the head's view that teachers were professionally qualified and if in their professional opinion a boy had committed an offence that justified caning, then that boy would be caned. Girls, however, were not caned. The reason was that they had not been caned at the girls' secondary modern school which had merged with the boys' secondary modern to form Southlands. At the time of the merger the head of the girls' school was appointed deputy head of the comprehensive and made it clear that neither she nor her staff would take up the cane.

Yet that day, corporal punishment had not only been raised as an issue; it had been raised by the deputy chairman of his governors, who must be at least thirty years younger than the head, and she had made the head look stupid and untruthful in front of his senior staff. It had started with this lady asking him what his policy was about corporal punishment. He had explained that he disliked the need for it, but considered that it must always be available as a last resort unless the authority was willing to provide a large number of special school places for disruptive pupils. The deputy chairman was a councillor and would know there was no prospect of this. He had justified the policy of no caning for girls on the grounds that introducing corporal punishment for girls, some of whom might even conceivably be married with children, was a retrograde step. Moreover, experience showed that girls could be dealt with successfully in other ways, while with boys a short, sharp shock was occasionally the best way to show them the error of their ways.

"Besides", he added, "a lot of boys would prefer something that's over quickly and recognise the fairness of it". His deputy chairman had replied mildly that she had always thought the point of punishment was that children should not like it. She then asked if she could see the punishment book, as a number of other governors had been asking about corporal punishment and were threatening to raise it as an issue at the next governors' meeting. "They're welcome to raise it; we've got nothing to hide", replied the head, "but here's the book".

He had been kicking himself for his confidence ever since. "But I don't think I understand", she had said as sweetly as ever. "You said it's only a last resort, but there are at least six children here who have been caned four times or more in the first two months of this term, and altogether there are some sixty names in the book. Isn't that rather a lot of last resorts?" His deputy and two senior mistresses who were present had come gallantly to the rescue, explaining that this had been an altogether exceptional term and they had had to stamp out epidemics of smoking and disruptive behaviour on the school bus. The boys who had been caned repeatedly were really exceptional cases and this was the only way to prevent their permanent suspension from the school.

These protestations hadn't helped, though. The deputy chairman still held the punishment book in her hands and took less than 30 seconds to establish that there had been a similar pattern in each of the previous four terms. "Well, I'll do what I can, headmaster", she said as she took her leave, "but I don't know if the chairman will be able to prevent the subject being raised in Any Other Business". The head wasn't impressed by her conciliatory tone, and cursed the Taylor Report which had led to the reorganisation of l.e.a.s' system for school management.

All the same, he realised that his governors made better allies than enemies, and the following day announced a review of the school's disciplinary procedures. The deputy head, Ron Jones, would enlist the help of any other teachers he thought necessary, and prepare a report for the head. He was to report how often each sanction was used, by whom and with what effect on subsequent behaviour.

The list of sanctions was well known. In theory sanctions escalated from a severe lecture, to lines or extra work, to a detention after school hours, to corporal punishment, to referral to the head or deputy, to exclusion or suspension. Exclusion or suspension could only be used by the head himself, and the authority's regulations forbade the use of corporal punishment by teachers with less than three years' experience. These teachers and all female teachers were expected to refer to the child's year tutor or to their own head of department when they thought this sanction necessary.

Ron Jones had a reputation in the staff room as something of a "yes" man. He did indeed give his head teacher loyal support, but privately thought the school's pastoral care and disciplinary systems hopelessly haphazard. Having been given the job of reviewing disciplinary procedures he decided that Tom Snelgrove needed a surprise. He enlisted the help of two year tutors, two heads of department and two young, relatively inexperienced teachers, one of whom was a union representative. Together they canvassed the whole staff, finding time in the course of the next three weeks for at least five minutes talk with each person about children whom they had punished, or for whom they had requested punishment, in the course of the previous week. Each teacher was also asked what other support he would have liked in dealing with the child.

The results were interesting. Many teachers seemed to prefer the use of lines to extra work, but it was fairly easy to predict who would prefer which sanction. About half the staff claimed seldom or never to use either. Several of the younger teachers and some of the older women felt strongly that there should be more back-up from the head of department and/or the year tutor, and that this would prevent the need for a lot of the petty punishments and for some of the canings. "We're each stuck in our little box and the kids know that unless it's a real emergency we'll deal with them ourselves, even if it does mean disrupting the whole lesson to do so", remarked one second year teacher. "If they thought that the senior and junior staff operated as a team and not as a crowd of individuals they would not play the system so much."

Most people thought corporal punishment for boys effective in the short term, but admitted that it seldom had any long-term effect; the same boys always seemed to come back for more. A few thought it should also be used on girls. One man remarked, "In fact, as far as I'm concerned you can abolish it for the boys and just keep it for some of those little cows in the third year – one of them is worse than all the boys put together".

The most disturbing thing to come out of the review, though not the least surprising to Ron Jones, was that most of the caning was done by, or at the request of, a small number of teachers. In fact, a quarter of the staff accounted for three-quarters of all canings. More to the point, three-quarters of all the children caned in the previous term had been caned more than once, and half had been caned three times or more. Moreover, three-quarters of all the children caned came from one small part of the catchment area which accounted for less than a quarter of the pupils on roll. The same trends were evident, to a slightly smaller degree with the other sanctions.

"We've always known that our problems come from the flats, but I'm a little surprised that it's as striking as that", said one of the year tutors. "I trust the pun wasn't intended", replied one of the scale I teachers, "but seriously, there are two things which come across to me from all this. The first is that we need a better pastoral care system for teachers, and the second is that we quite obviously aren't having any effect on the children from the flats, except perhaps to harden them in their rejection of schools."

"In the present financial situation there's no chance of the authority giving us any extra money to cater for these children", remarked Ron Jones, "so we'll have to do the best we can ourselves. I'll draft something which we can all discuss before it goes to the head."

Ron Jones' draft proposals were scarcely radical, but did involve quite substantial changes by the standards of Southlands Secondary School. He proposed that caning should only be inflicted with the permission of the head, deputy, year tutor or one of the four heads of subject faculties. He also agreed that the job description of the heads of department should explicitly include responsibility for initial investigation of disciplinary problems within their departments.

Ron proposed that he himself should assume responsibility for support and in-service training of probationary teachers. He also suggested a general tightening-up of the procedures for giving detention; the name of the teacher giving the detention should be noted in the detention book as well as the name of the pupil. In this way he would be alerted to any teacher who was referring children unusually often and could investigate whether additional support was needed. Staff were to be required to give children work to do during their detentions and were to be discouraged from giving lines as an alternative. The names of all children punished would be co-ordinated once a week by Ron himself, before the weekly welfare meeting with the education welfare officer and the year tutors.

The proposals were accepted by the other teachers involved in the review. Tom Snelgrove read them and remarked dryly that Ron seemed to be taking a lot on himself, but it all seemed sensible enough to him. "Now", said Tom as his deputy was about to leave, "would you mind producing two summaries of this paper, one for all the staff, and the second for the governors. You know the sort of thing — something intelligible to five year olds! But there's one thing I'd like you to add. Say that there's no policy against caning girls; just say it hasn't been necessary so far." That, he thought to himself, should keep the deputy chairman of his governors thinking!

Questions

1 Comment on the policy of caning boys but not girls. (Is this a case for the Equal Opportunities Commission?)

2 Can the fact that children prefer it, ever be a justification for punishment (of any kind)?

3 Could the head have refused to let the deputy chairman of his governors see his punishment book? If he had refused, how might she still have obtained the information she wanted?

4 What does the information from the punishment book tell you about the school and its policies?

5 Comment on the usual escalation of sanctions at Southlands School.

6 Comment on the use of lines and/or extra work as sanctions. What are the arguments for and against each?

7 Do you agree that greater back-up from senior staff would reduce the need for corporal punishment? Might it simply reduce the subject teacher's own commitment to deal with the problem himself?

8 Is corporal punishment different from any other form of punishment in having a short-term effect but no long-term effect?

9 What do you think of Ron Jones' proposals? Do you think they were too radical, or not radical enough, from what you know of the school?

10 What general problems might the head and deputy encounter in implementing the proposals? How could these problems be overcome?
11 Describe in detail the stages in which you think Ron Jones' proposals should be implemented. What preliminary discussions are needed with heads of department, year tutors, other staff, parents and/or pupils? What sort of time-scale would you envisage?

Peter

Main themes

1 Case conferences are sometimes more valuable in reducing the anxiety of professional personnel who attend them than in helping the children who are under discussion.

2 The school system sometimes makes unreasonable demands on children – and also on teachers and social workers.

3 School policy and children often interact to create problems that are at least as serious for teachers as for children.

Enquiries from outside agencies about boys were channelled routinely to Ron Jones; inquiries about girls went to a senior mistress. This time it was a social worker ringing about Peter Waddon. At the school's insistence, the authority had taken Peter to the juvenile court on the grounds of persistent truancy. Having the parents fined under Section 40 of the 1944 Act had no effect, since the fine was, allegedly, paid by social security. The authority had naturally asked the juvenile court to make a Care Order on Peter. Just as naturally, thought Ron Jones dryly, the magistrates had accepted the recommendation of the social services department's social worker that a Supervision Order would be adequate.

Ron wasn't really quite sure why they had pressed for action against Peter. What he had seen of the local children's homes did not lead him to expect that Peter would be helped if he was placed in one of them. He seldom attended school, which was quite a relief because he was such a nuisance when he did turn up. Several of the staff were quite open in hoping that Peter would continue to truant – which exasperated the education welfare officer who was under pressure from the head and deputy head to get him back, and had made strenuous efforts to achieve his return.

Now, however, the court had made a social worker responsible for Peter's supervision and the education welfare officer (e.w.o.), with a mixture of resentment and relief, could turn his attention elsewhere. Jim Hudson, the social worker was ringing about a case conference the following Thursday when the agencies involved with the Waddon family, including teachers from the children's school, were meeting to discuss what to do about a case of possible battering against a younger child. "It's a foregone conclusion really", sighed

108

Ron Jones, "we'll all agree to keep our eyes open and our fingers crossed, and go away thankful that so many other people are involved". Jim Hudson's question, though, was more pressing. Would Mr Jones be willing to discuss Peter Waddon's attendance and behaviour at the same meeting?

The first 45 minutes of the conference went more or less as Ron had predicted. Everyone expressed their anxieties about the Waddon children, but no one, apart from the e.w.o. and a primary school class teacher, had seen any signs of physical injury on any of the children. The one injury the primary school class teacher had noticed was bruising on the leg of an eight-year-old boy, which apparently had been done by dad when Alfie had come home late after playing out. The conference fizzled out when the educational psychologist rather tactlessly asked the e.w.o whether he thought the bruising was more or less severe than would be inflicted by a cane at school − and the e.w.o. had to admit that there probably wasn't much in it (though the primary school head had quickly and indignantly denied that any children were ever caned at her school).

Jim Hudson, Ron Jones and Peter's year tutor continued the meeting on their own. Jim explained that as Peter's social worker he was naturally very concerned about the question of his attendance. But although Peter's truancy was the reason for the Supervision Order being made, his own responsibility as a social worker was by no means confined to school attendance. Nevertheless, he had been discussing a return to school with Peter, who made it clear that he saw no point. "He says that when he returned to school the day after his dad got done for £25 in the magistrates court for him wagging school, the first thing he got was a caning for wagging it!" What Jim Hudson thought it better not to add was Peter's defiant insistence that Ron Jones' caning had not been nearly as bad as his dad's belting. "Another thing he claims", continued Jim, "is that he can't do the work, and even if he did attend all the time he still wouldn't get any help. He says he just has to sit at the back; then he gets bored; then he gets some more stick, so he starts wagging school again!"

"I hope you don't think I'm being critical", Jim Hudson concluded to the increasingly resentful teachers. "Just tell me you never use corporal punishment and I'll be only too delighted to go back and give him a bollocking for telling me a pack of lies!"

The trouble, of course, was that it wasn't a pack of lies. Peter had been caned for truancy on returning to school the day after his father had been fined. The point was that Ron Jones had no idea that the case had been heard. Having established that Peter's absence was due to persistent truancy and that he had also encouraged three other boys to truant, he simply administered the routine punishment. In addition, Peter had a reading age of less than eight, and Southlands had no special remedial provision in the fourth and fifth years. The theory was that the remedial department would, quite literally, remedy any learning difficulties in the first three years, and by the fourth all pupils would have achieved an adequate level of literacy to cope satisfactorily with the options system leading to CSE examinations. On the whole the theory worked very well, but it fell down with boys like Peter who had been absent more often than they were present.

So it was quite possible, Ron Jones had to concede, that Peter sat uncomprehendingly at the back of the class. He was never a major problem in school, but there were lots of minor incidents which had a cumulative effect. He had indeed been caned on a number of occasions for offences ranging from "accidentally" pushing over his desk, to smoking in the toilets, to encouraging other pupils to skip lessons.

Jim Hudson agreed that Peter's poor attainments and his boredom in school might well be his own fault. But as the supervisory social worker, he did not feel justified in taking Peter back to court for truanting from a school which, for whatever reason, was offering him an education which he could not possibly cope with. At Peter's age, special education was out of the question, so was there absolutely no chance of giving him any extra help in the remedial department, if only once or twice a week? Privately Ron Jones thought there was no chance on earth but the meeting ended with vague promises that Jim would do his best to get Peter back to school, and Ron would see what could be arranged at school.

As Ron had expected, the remedial department absolutely refused to take Peter, not least because they remembered him as a poor attender who was troublesome when he did turn up. Nevertheless, an assistant year tutor did agree to take an interest in him and to see him twice a week in his free periods for counselling and remedial reading. Things seemed to be working out well. Peter got on well with Gill Barber, and also seemed to be making a good relationship with his social worker. Both emphasised to him that only he could make decisions about his future.

Whether it was the extra confidence he got from his relationship with Gill Barber and Jim Hudson, or whether it would have happened anyway, was a matter for some speculation in the staff room, but after six weeks Peter was seen smoking outside the school gate after school hours. He was told he would be caned for this, but refused to accept the punishment. He was taken to the head, who warned him that his refusal would lead to his exclusion from school. He still refused, so was excluded. His father backed him in his refusal, and Jim Hudson decided, after an unpleasant meeting with the head, not to take further action. Whatever the rights or wrongs of the case, there was no point in seeking a Care Order on a boy with less than six months left at school.

The head and Ron Jones might have felt quite relieved to be rid of Peter, but there was a sequel. A week later four more fifth year pupils were seen smoking outside the school gate, this time during school hours. They all refused to accept corporal punishment and were promptly excluded. The parents of two of the boys decided to cut their losses — neither boy was taking any exams — and did not insist on their returning to school to receive punishment. The head asked the authority to prosecute the parents for their children's failure to attend school, an action which he knew to be legally quite possible in the circumstances. The authority refused, and the head was left wondering how on earth he had let himself be manoeuvred into such a loser's position.

Questions

1 Is it possible for a fine to be paid by social security? How else might the Education Department (or the Magistrates) expect parents who are receiving social security to pay the fines imposed?

2 Do you see any point in legal action against parents over poor attendance (as opposed to legal action in connection with the children themselves)?

3 What are the disadvantages of legal action against: (i) parents, and (ii) children?

4 Was the educational psychologist's question at the case conference unfair? Is there ever a case for removing a child from home on the grounds of injuries less severe than would be inflicted by a caning? What is "reasonable" punishment: (i) at school, and (ii) at home?

5 In the teacher's position, how would you have reacted to Jim Hudson's questions? How do you think you should have reacted?

6 What is the point in caning a boy like Peter?

7 Do you think the remedial department's attitude was unreasonable?

8 Was Jim Hudson reasonable in making clear at his meeting with the teachers that he would not take Peter back to court for refusing to attend a school that was not meeting his educational needs?

9 How would you organise the remedial reading and counselling sessions which the assistant year tutor offered Peter? How would you combine remedial reading and counselling? How would you set about assessing his "remedial" needs?

10 Were the assistant year tutor and social worker right (or accurate) in telling Peter that only he could make decisions about his future?

11 Did the school have any justification in trying to cane Peter for smoking outside the school gate after school hours? What is the legal position in a case of this sort?

12 What is the legal position if a pupil refuses corporal punishment?

13 Do you agree with Jim Hudson's refusal to take no further action?

14 What does the sequel tell you about the attitude of pupils (and staff) at the school?

15 Could the head manoeuvre himself out of his "loser's position" without losing face?

Newlands Comprehensive School

Main themes
1 Pupils from one section of a school's catchment area may create most of the behavioural and educational problems.

2 If a behavioural unit is to be effective, the details have to be thought out carefully in the light of the social and educational climate in the staff room.

The head of Newlands Comprehensive School read the report of the study group he had set up with mixed feelings. Part of their brief was to consider whether the school needed to make additional provision for its disruptive pupils. With official recognition from the D.E.S. in the form of a small booklet, special units were becoming popular.

Sam Griffith's school served a well-to-do middle-class area on the edge of a medium-sized city. About a quarter of the children, however, came from a run-down council estate. The school had a thoroughly comprehensive intake, covering the whole spectrum from extreme affluence to extreme poverty. In theory this pleased Sam, but he realised that in practice the middle-class mores of the majority made it more difficult to cater for the minority. The school had high academic standards, and the number of requests for a place there, shown by the authority's parental choice system for secondary schools, far exceeded the number of places.

Unfortunately, the staff room contained a division almost as profound as that in the catchment area. Most of the older teachers had spent their early years in the profession in the grammar school system and viewed the apathy, indifference and occasional defiance or disruption of the minority with a kind of bewildered horror. A number of younger teachers, on the other hand, made little secret of their view that the school was unduly influenced by the aspirations of middle-class parents and was falling down in its responsibility towards working-class children. Sam Griffith realised that he had only himself to thank for this; he had urged the appointment of the teachers concerned, against the advice of his colleagues, because he felt that they would inject new ideas and new attitudes. He had been right, but the effect had been divisive.

The problem, predictably enough, lay in the disproportionate number of children from Highbrook Estate who were sent to senior staff for disrupting normal lessons and other offences. It not only offended the social conscience of the younger teachers that almost all corporal punishment in the school was inflicted on Highbrook Estate children, it offended Sam Griffith's as well. The problem came to a head through a casual encounter in the pub with the head of the local school for maladjusted children. "You give us some right cases from Highbrook Estate", he had remarked thoughtfully. "It's funny that we get more kids from that estate than from all the others in the authority put together. I was asking a friend from the University about it; he's been working on the census and he couldn't see anything special about it!" "Don't tell me", Sam replied, "it's the school — cheers!" and he got up to buy his colleague a drink.

This might not have mattered too much if his deputy had not come in the following day with a story of a similar chance encounter with the head of one of the authority's two schools for ESN(M) pupils, who had said more or less the same thing.

The study group which Sam Griffith set up contained the assistant head responsible for curriculum development and the time-table, two year tutors and one other senior teacher, with the deputy head as chairman. They were given a term to prepare their report and were told to visit other schools which might have had useful experiences. The group had indeed visited four other schools, all of which had established "behavioural units" of one kind or another. They had not thought it worthwhile to visit two other schools whose head teachers had gone on record as opposing the establishment of special units on both practical and philosophical grounds.

The study group's report advocated no major changes in the school's existing systems of pastoral care and discipline. They considered the possibility of appointing a school counsellor but rejected it on the grounds that the problems facing the school were not the sort that could be solved simply by personal counselling. This approach might, they thought, be useful for withdrawn children or for children with emotional problems arising from relationships at home, but it did not seem very relevant to the problem of disruption in the classroom and during the lunch hour. Sam agreed with the conclusion, but not with the reasoning. "For goodness sake", he murmured, "they ought to know by now that all the children we're worried about have all sorts of problems at home, not least in their relationships with their parents".

Another possibility considered was the extension of the school's remedial department to include an all-age class specifically for pupils whose poor behaviour was related to low educational attainments. The argument was that almost all the school's difficult children were educationally backward, and if this could be rectified their behaviour would improve. The flaw in this reasoning, the study group pointed out, was that a lot of the disturbing pupils appeared educationally retarded *because* of their disruptive behaviour, not the other way round. Moreover, it was thought that the scheme would disrupt the remedial department which was starting to achieve good results after a difficult period due to staff changes.

The eventual decision was to recommend opening a special unit for pupils who were continually disruptive in normal lessons or presented any other exceptional difficulties of behaviour. The unit would be located in a large classroom near the science laboratories. One teacher should be responsible for it, with the help of three or four others who would each take a few sessions, totalling an equivalent of 1.5 teachers. Selection would be at the discretion of the head and/or deputy, following full discussions with the year tutor, class teacher and anyone else with knowledge of the child.

Length of stay was to be flexible, but there should be a clear expectation that each child should return to normal lessons as quickly as possible. In most cases it was expected that the return to ordinary classes would be phased, with the teacher in charge negotiating the child's initial return to lessons in which he was likely to succeed. The unit would cater for boys and girls. There would be no maximum or minimum numbers, though the upper limit would naturally be restricted by the need for a small group.

The regime should not, the report continued, be punitive, but nor should the unit be seen as an easy alternative to normal lessons. Experience in other schools suggested that few, if any, children would actively seek admission, even to the most permissive unit, but once there it was often difficult to persuade them to return to ordinary lessons. "To maintain the continuity of the curriculum", the deputy had noted, "it may be desirable to encourage subject teachers to set children work to carry out under the unit teacher's supervision, which they would normally have been doing in their regular class".

With regard to staffing and finance, the study group suggested that the authority be approached with a request for one teacher above establishment. The remaining half a teacher recommended in the report could be provided from the school's resources. It was thought that no extensive funds would be needed to open the unit; a capital outlay of £500 should cover it, with annual running costs to be negotiated from the school's capitation allowance thereafter.

Three things worried Sam Griffith. First, he suspected that a flexible length of stay would mean an indefinite length of stay for several children. Second, he knew certain of his staff well enough to have faint hope in the idea of "encouraging subject teachers to set children work to carry out under the unit teacher's supervision". Once a child entered the unit there would be an understandable temptation to forget about him and give the remaining pupils some much-needed attention. Finally, he felt certain that the unit would cater exclusively for children from Highbrook Estate, thus accentuating the sort of division he most wanted to avoid.

On the other hand, there was a pressing need for some sort of action, and Sam found himself wavering between two possibilities. The first was to open a unit, but on a much more structured basis which would guarantee a child's return to ordinary lessons. There would be no nonsense about flexible lengths of stay. Instead there would be a maximum length of three weeks. Teachers would not be encouraged to set children work to carry out whilst in the unit — they would be required to do so. On return, pupils would be closely supervised through the daily report system. Discipline in the unit would be tight and pupils would be expected to work hard and continuously.

The second possibility was for a more child-centred sort of unit which would

114

aim to provide some disturbed pupils with an educational alternative to ordinary classroom lessons. Length of stay would be at least a term and probably more than a year in most cases. The emphasis would be on helping the selected pupils to acquire greater self-confidence, and to cope more satisfactorily with the difficulties they experience both at home and at school.

The first possibility, Sam realised could be seen as a form of support for staff, the second as a form of treatment for children. The advantage of the first was that its structure required close integration into the mainstream of the school, and prevented teachers using the unit as a long-term "dump". The disadvantages lay in: (i) its inherently punitive nature; (ii) the unsatisfactory public image that could result from its exclusive intake of Highbrook Estate pupils; (iii) the fact that its structure would make investigation and treatment of the family or psychological problems which led to the disruptive behaviour in the first place, virtually impossible.

The advantages of the second possibility lay in the possibility of doing something to help the school's most troublesome, and usually least successful pupils, while at the same time removing their disruptive influence on ordinary classes for a prolonged period. The disadvantages lay in: (i) the difficulty of returning a child to ordinary lessons after a prolonged period in the unit; (ii) the small number of pupils that the unit would be able to accept; (iii) the strong possibility that treatment would be ineffective; (iv) the objection that a unit of this sort would be trying to do, on a shoe-string, what the special schools were much better qualified to do already.

The study group's proposals, the head felt, fell between two stools; they paid lip service to the idea of treatment, without thinking out the implications. Reluctantly, he found himself accepting the idea of a unit as inevitable. He did not feel that his own background equipped him to advise, let alone dictate, what form it should take, but he did feel certain that the study group's ideas needed to be tightened up if the idea was to result in a successful venture.

Questions

1 Can you comment further on the problems inherent in a fully comprehensive intake, from extreme affluence to extreme poverty? What are the advantages of this sort of intake? How can the difficulties be overcome?

2 Do you agree with the head's method of injecting new ideas and new attitudes? How might he have reduced the resulting division in the staff room?

3 Should the authority have made it clear to the head that he was referring a disproportionate number of children to special schools? What pressure could the authority have brought to bear? What help might it have offered?

4 Have you any views on the study group's composition? Should it have included some younger, probably less experienced teachers?

5 Why do you think they decided not to visit the schools known to be opposed to the idea of behavioural units?

6 Do you think the study group's arguments for rejecting the idea of a school counsellor were correct?

7 Do you agree with their argument against extending the remedial department?

8 Do you think the study group's staffing proposals for a unit were adequate?

9 Do you agree with Sam Griffith's three reservations? Can you think of any further problems in the study group's proposals?

10 Do you see the alternatives in the same clear-cut way as the head? Can the two aims of support for staff and treatment for children be reconciled?

11 Was the idea of a unit really inevitable? What other possibilities might the head have explored – perhaps before setting up the study group?

Simon

Main themes

1 A behavioural unit can sometimes offer long-term support by taking children on a strictly part-time basis.

2 Some children try to use a unit as a long-term sanctuary, to insulate themselves from the demands of day-to-day school life.

3 A crucial decision in counselling and pastoral care, as in teaching, is when to put pressure on children.

Newlands School opened its unit eighteen months after the study group's first report to Sam Griffith. His criticisms had not been resented by his colleagues; they did not expect to persuade him easily. Yet nor did they altogether accept that their original ideas fell between two stools. Providing an additional resource for teachers, whose lessons were being filled with lead in ten seconds flat by the school's most disruptive marksmen, was not necessarily inconsistent with the idea of helping these pupils to become more acceptable members of society. The head's ideas of a short-term "sin-bin" and a long-term "head-case" unit were both unnecessarily extreme.

Sam Griffith read their second report with satisfaction. He had provoked them into thinking for themselves! The unit, when it opened, seemed to him a well thought out compromise. No children were to attend full-time except for a maximum of two weeks, and then only in exceptional circumstances. On the other hand, once a child was accepted it was expected that he would maintain contact with the unit for at least a term and probably over a year.

The majority would start by attending the unit for half to three-quarters of their time-table, gradually reducing this to between a quarter and a half after a term or two. Admission was on the recommendation of the pastoral care committee, chaired by the head, but the final decision was to remain with the teacher in charge of the unit. If he felt he could do nothing to help a child, or if a child's admission at a particular time would upset the progress of other children, this was to be respected.

The unit premises had been subdivided to provide a quiet area with second-hand armchairs, a carpet, sink and facilities for making coffee or tea, and a teaching area with blackboard and desks. The original staffing recommendation had been modified; the teacher in charge now had an assistant, who spent half his time in the unit. The teacher in charge was a brisk, no-nonsense, middle-aged lady who had been a highly successful year tutor and a less successful PE teacher. "I'm too old and too fat for PE", she told the head at her interview, "and I'm damned if I'm going to diet if I don't get this job, so I'll become even less use at PE!"

The curriculum was critically described by a visiting HMI as a mixture between a secondary school remedial department and a primary school integrated day. Helen Lipton was, in fact, an able remedial teacher as well as a PE specialist, but much of her teaching was based on project work arising from the children's own interests or from work they had already done in the unit. Her basic aim was to ensure that no pupil should leave the unit without the elementary reading and writing ability to cope with ordinary lessons. Of course, preparatory work would be needed to ensure that they would also understand the lessons, but that bridge could be crossed when it was reached.

The pupils ranged in age from the first to the fourth year. Helen Lipton refused to admit fifth year pupils unless they had already passed through the unit. She never allowed more than eight at a time and preferred to confine the number to six. Continuing attendance at some ordinary lessons was seldom too much of a problem, since almost all children were able to get on successfully with one or two teachers. It raised difficulties with one or two persistent poor attenders, for whom the unit was a sort of half-way house back to ordinary lessons but with these children Helen was able to arrange for an official "blind eye" to be turned when their initial return to school was on a part-time basis to attend the unit.

Most of the other teachers agreed with Helen Lipton that the unit was benefiting the school and the children who attended it. Yet Simon was an exception. He was too small and too quiet to be considered an outright failure, but he was certainly not improving. The reason for his referral was an accumulation of problems. He had truanted at least twice a week, usually, it seemed, to avoid PE and maths; in school he was a social isolate, with no particular enemies and no friends; his behaviour was not severely disruptive, but he was a nuisance in all lessons. The sort of things his teachers complained about were dreaming, putting other children off their work, inattention, asking silly questions and reluctance to work.

Simon was next to the youngest in a large family living at Highbrook Estate, the problem area of the school's intake. His older brothers and sisters had led undistinguished, but not disastrous, careers at school and Simon was not really much worse. Helen Lipton supposed he had really been referred because people felt something ought to be done about the Welbourns and the unit seemed worth a try. Both parents were out of work and took for granted that the authorities would complain about their children. Taking the steam out of these complaints took up much of the parents' energy, but they seemed to have been quite successful since none of the children had so far been taken from home by the courts.

Helen Lipton saw Simon as a neglected younger child in a rather neglected family. She regarded the purpose of his admission to the unit as building up his self-confidence to enable him to make conscious decisions for himself. On admission, she thought, he was simply drifting into whatever course of action seemed easiest. Thus, it was easier not to try to make progress with his reading than to try, and risk failure; it was easier to truant on PE days than to attend and risk the teacher's wrath because he had no kit, or unwashed kit; it was easier to wrap himself in a cocoon of indifference to other children than to talk or play with them and risk rebuff.

The problem areas, therefore, were his educational backwardness and his social interaction both with other children and with adults. There was no specific perceptual difficulty to explain his reading failure; it seemed the predictable result of eight years poor attendance at school, combined with a consistent lack of success when he did attend. Helen drew up a remedial reading programme which combined the use of the Syncrofax individual learning machine with word games such as junior Scrabble and word Lotto, which had to be played with two or three other children. In this way she hoped not only to overcome Simon's aversion to reading, by avoiding the use of books with which he had been failing for so long; she also hoped he would become more confident in his social behaviour with other children.

The plan had seemed sensible enough, yet after a year Helen Lipton had to admit that it was not really working. Admittedly Simon had made eighteen months progress in his reading age but, even so, he was still only reading at the level of the average nine and a half-year-old. He was also attending his 25 per cent of ordinary lessons as much as he skipped them – an improvement which was lost on the art, RE and social studies teachers who had reluctantly agreed to retain him in their lessons. On the other hand, he was as much of a nuisance as ever when he did attend. Moreover, his lack of self-confidence and associated tendency to take the easy way out, seemed if anything even more noticeable.

It was not, Helen thought, that he had developed from a withdrawn state into an aggressive one, as some children did; nor could his lack of progress be attributed to deterioration in the family's circumstances. It all came down to the fact that he was using the unit passively, as a kind of sanctuary, and not as a place which would help him cope with the day-to-day demands of ordinary school life. Helen had always believed that some children needed "tea and sympathy", but when tea and sympathy became a substitute for ordinary existence, it was time to call a halt.

Her colleague took an even more pessimistic view. He argued that admitting Simon to the unit had confirmed his image of himself as a bit of a failure who could not be expected to do the same things as other children. "I don't think it mattered very much what we did with Simon", he explained. "The point is that by accepting him we justified his belief that the easy solution is the only solution. The trouble is we were, and are, bound to fail, because if we push him back into ordinary lessons he will just stop attending school altogether."

"I think that's what we'll do all the same", said Helen. "We don't know that he'll stop attending school altogether, but we do know that he's just drifting with us, taking up a place we could offer someone else; and we also know that his aimlessness is starting to affect two of the other children. It's time to put pressure on Simon."

Questions

1 Do you think the revised proposals for the unit constitute an improvement over the original ones?

2 Do you believe that the head's intention was to provoke the teachers in the original study group to think for themselves?

3 Do you think it makes better sense to have a full-time teacher and one half-timer, than a full-time teacher and three or four part-timers? What are the advantages and disadvantages of each?

4 Have you any comments about the unit premises?

5 What would be Helen Lipton's reasons for refusing to admit fifth year pupils unless they had already passed through the unit? Do you agree with them?

6 Are the unit numbers reasonable? How would the unit teachers get over possible criticism that they had an "easy number" with so few pupils?

7 Can you think of any pupils you have taught who drift in the way Helen Lipton considered Simon a drifter? Does her assessment ring true?

8 Can you think of ways to tackle the problem, apart from the ones Helen Lipton suggested?

9 Helen Lipton was unimpressed by the improvements in Simon's reading and in his attendance. Was she expecting too much too quickly?

10 Can you think of children who have used a behavioural unit, or counselling sessions "passively, as a kind of sanctuary, and not as a place to help them cope with the day-to-day demands of ordinary school life"? Do you think this is a reasonable use of the facility for Simon – or for your own pupils?

11 Do you think the pessimism of Helen Lipton's colleagues was justified?

12 What sorts of pressure might Helen Lipton have put on Simon? How?

Henry Beardsley C. of E. Comprehensive School

Main themes

1 Pastoral care must not depend too heavily on the quality of a few individuals.

2 The class teacher must be the basic unit of pastoral care, but this role is sometimes made impossible by the school's organisation.

3 Good pastoral care implies oversight of and concern for the child's educational progress, not simply concern about "problems".

Henry Beardsley Church of England Comprehensive School had been opened by the Reverend Doctor Henry Beardsley himself, on the occasion of his retirement from a distinguished career in public and ecclesiastical life. Situated in the middle of the most depressed and depressing area of inner-city dereliction in a large industrial town, the new school rose above its grimy surroundings like a glass and concrete giant − "Or you could say simply that it stands out like a sore thumb", the reverend doctor remarked privately to his wife and children. The comprehensive school was formed from five secondary moderns and a small, run-down grammar school.

Emma Curtis' appointment as head had taken the profession by surprise. They had assumed that only a man could cope with the district's tarmac and concrete desert − jungle would hardly be the appropriate word. They had been wrong. Emma Curtis rapidly proved herself as efficient in organising her staff as in disciplining the school's most difficult pupils. Two things had attracted the attention of the selection committee at her appointment interview. First, her uncompromising insistence that inner-city dereliction and high educational standards were not a contradiction in terms; and second, the evidence that she had already made her ideas work during her three years as deputy head of a London school where the head was slowly dying of cancer.

It was sometimes said in the staff room that Emma Curtis did not care much about pastoral care. This was untrue; it was simply that she didn't talk much about it. Her priority lay in proving to the school's children, including those from the most deprived homes, that they could achieve things of which they − and their parents − could be proud. Teachers who achieved good results received unlimited encouragement; those who did not were made aware of the fact. The school's achievements were widely recognised; parents came to open evenings, plays and concerts in numbers unheard of at any of the old secondary modern schools. Traditionalists in the office and on the Education Committee complained from time to time, particularly when a quarter of the entries for an exhibition of fifth year pupils' paintings were nudes, and again when Emma invited a famous — or notorious — communist trade union leader to be guest speaker on speech day and he had denounced the whole Education Committee as capitalist lackeys. They had to admit, though, that the art exhibition had received favourable reviews in *The Times* and the *Daily Telegraph*, and the previous year's speech day guest had been a right-wing Tory.

Pastoral care was organised conventionally, but with Emma Curtis's usual meticulous attention to detail. She believed firmly that the five year tutors must all be independent-minded people, able to see a child's point of view, capable of putting it to their colleagues, and able to command the respect and confidence of the parents as well as of the children. Her insistence that year tutors should do home visits had annoyed the school's education welfare officer (e.w.o), who believed teachers were untrained for work with parents. Emma did not tolerate demarcation disputes gladly. "Some time", she told him acidly, "you must tell me about your own training, and then you can tell me how you plan to fit in all the year tutors' visits as well as your own!"

Fortunately, the e.w.o., as Emma had already realised, was a mature enough man to recognise the truth in her reply; he also recognised that all five year tutors were good at their job. It was largely due to them that the school had developed a reputation amongst parents for listening to any worries or complaints, investigating them carefully, and when necessary acting on them.

The division between pastoral staff and subject specialists appeared not to cause any problems at Henry Beardsley School. This was as much due to the staff room ethos inculcated by the head, as to the organisation of pastoral care. The gap was, however, also eased by the fact that a senior member of the remedial department was one of the year tutors. Nor was there any nonsense about pastoral care staff not being involved with discipline. In emergencies, which were few, they would deal with disruptive behaviour themselves, but more often would discuss the child's management with the teacher and head of department concerned, and come to an agreement with them.

Yet Emma Curtis remained unsatisfied. The system was working well, but it depended too heavily on the five exceptional people she had been able to appoint to the year tutor jobs. Any one of them could apply, and probably should have applied, for a deputy headship by now.

More important, she recognised that while the year tutors did a remarkably good job with a minority of particularly difficult children, they could do no more than oversee the progress of the ordinary majority. Recently she had seen growing evidence that some children were failing to fulfil their potential, even though they gave no outward cause for concern. A number of small things had attracted her attention. For example, the head of a local primary school had expressed mild surprise that a former star pupil did not seem to have achieved anything special in his secondary school career; then the local child guidance clinic had rung up for information about a child referred to them by a GP and she found she had embarrassingly little to tell them after circulating all teachers who knew the boy; then a mother had pointed out, just as her son was about to leave, that of course his work had fallen off since his father left them, and wasn't it a pity.

In theory, the person who should have been able to give information about all these children was the class teacher. In theory, the class teacher was the basic unit of pastoral care, who would refer anything out of the ordinary to the year tutor, who had the time and the experience to investigate and deal with them. In practice, Emma reflected, the class teachers had something in common with the curate's egg — good in parts. Their job description made clear that they should look for evidence of uneven attainments, poor homework, or erratic performance generally. In practice they seldom referred children to the year tutors, and those they did refer were the obvious ones who had already been spotted by other teachers.

The class teachers each saw their class twice a day for ten minutes, for registration. They also took their class for at least one "class period" a week, which could be used as they saw fit. Children had one class teacher in their first year, when it was felt they needed special help in settling, another for the next two years, and a third for the last two years. This reflected the academic organisation of the school, based on a group of three to four teachers per class in the first year, a fairly traditional secondary school curriculum, though on a strictly-mixed ability basis in the second and third years, and a guided option system for the final two.

Emma Curtis thought she identified two distinct problems. First, it was accepted in theory, but not in practice, that class teachers had a responsibility for pastoral care. Second, it was difficult for the best class teacher to get to know his pupils well enough to monitor all aspects of their progress when he might only teach them for one lesson a week. Third, the year tutors' job description emphasised their responsibility in liaising with other teachers to produce the best possible treatment for each child. It mentioned class teachers specifically, but said nothing about any responsibility for co-ordinating the work of class teachers.

"In other words", Emma concluded her opening remarks at the fortnightly year tutors' meeting, "I think we now have a system of pastoral care that caters admirably for the exceptional child. I think the ordinary child is also catered for well, in most cases, by the quality of teaching in the subject departments. The children I'm worried about are the ordinary children who slip through the net without, if I may mix my metaphors, a ripple. The next stage, then, it seems to me, is to raise the quality of pastoral care for ordinary children to the same high level as you now provide for the problem children. Unless anyone has a better idea, this seems to imply an upgrading of the pastoral responsibilities of class teachers. I would be glad of your views at our next meeting on how this might be achieved."

The year tutors met four times before the next fortnightly meeting to discuss the head's request. They weren't really surprised by it as they were all aware of the limitations in the class teacher system and knew that the school must be failing to recognise some children's needs. On the other hand, they valued their own ability to negotiate with any of their colleagues on the way a particular child should be handled; this enabled them to place pastoral care where it belonged — in the classroom.

At the next meeting with the head they made six recommendations: (i) that a class teacher should stay with his class throughout the whole of their school career until they reached school leaving age; (ii) that a class teacher's responsibility should, if possible, be voluntary; (iii) that it should be stated to all staff, that initial inquiries about any child who gives them cause for concern should be directed to the class teacher, and that senior staff should support this by refusing to accept direct referrals except in an emergency; (iv) that class teachers should be responsible for ensuring collection of all homework, for reporting missing or incomplete work to the appropriate teacher, and for ensuring that the work is completed at a later date; (v) that each year tutor should have responsibility for co-ordinating the work of all class teachers in his year; (vi) that there should be weekly "year meetings" between each year tutor and his class teachers while the head was taking assembly.

"I'm not quite sure that I like your kind gift of five assemblies a week", said Emma Curtis carefully, "but the general proposals are in line with my own thinking. Perhaps we could look at the details now".

Questions

1 Is there any sense in which a school like Henry Beardsley can be called comprehensive?
2 Had the traditionalists in the office and on the Education Committee anything to complain about?
3 Comment on the qualities the head expected of the five year tutors. Did she have her priorities right?
4 In what circumstances do you think teachers should do home visits? Did the e.w.o. have any justification for his annoyance?
5 Is there any justification for a division between pastoral and disciplinary responsibilities?
6 Do you think the head of department should be involved in discussions with members of his department about the management of a difficult child, or should he confine his attention to the curriculum?

7 Emma Curtis had recently been given three examples of children "slipping through the net" without being known well by any teacher. How far is this inevitable in a large school?
8 Do you agree with the head's conclusion about the need to upgrade the pastoral responsibility of class teachers?
9 Are the year tutors right in their assumption that pastoral care should be put "where it belongs — in the classroom"?
10 What are the strengths and weaknesses of the year tutors' six recommendations? How could the weaknesses be overcome?
11 How would you set about implementing the recommendations?

Jane

Main themes

1 Children who appear least upset by the death of a close relative are often the most severely affected.

2 Difficult behaviour may start for one reason and continue for another; finding the original cause will not necessarily help in finding a solution.

Jane Hudson was one of Henry Beardsley School's few undoubted failures. Her career there culminated with the dubious distinction of being the first girl ever to be suspended — the authority's euphemism for expelled. The incident which led to her suspension was serious enough; she had held a first year girl's head under the water in a handbasin until she was nearly unconscious, and then punched the teacher who had dragged her away, in the mouth, breaking two teeth. The first year girl's offence was accidentally bumping into Jane as she ran into the toilets.

Yet this incident on its own would never have been considered serious enough to warrant suspension. It was merely the last in a long list of antisocial acts, each of which marked Jane out as a girl ready, willing and eager to challenge anyone and anything in authority. "Would anyone like to swop one antisocial girl for a dozen antisocial boys?" her long-suffering year tutor had once asked in despair.

Jane's family was well known. "I don't *like* either of her parents", the same year tutor explained to Emma Curtis, the head, "but there's no way I can blame *them* for all that she's done!" Her father was a brusque, authoritarian warehouse foreman. He had spent twenty years in the army, leaving when Jane, his only child, was seven years old. He had liked the army life and admired army discipline, but left at his wife's insistence in order to give his family a more settled life. Apart from his endless problems with Jane he had no regrets at leaving the army. Mrs Hudson was a conscientious, rather plaintive woman who kept her home spotlessly clean, and accepted unquestioningly her husband's rather Victorian views about a woman's role in the home. She would never stand up to her husband, but in minor things had been known to cover up for Jane. This never happened with anything important though, and Jane knew better

124

than to even try to persuade her mother not to tell her father about her many serious offences.

Discipline in the home seemed to be extremely strict, fairly constant and totally ineffective. In fairness, the moderate consistency was almost certainly due to the total ineffectiveness. Mr Hudson had thrashed Jane with a leather belt on numerous occasions in the four years since she had been a pupil at Henry Beardsley School. Yet even he realised that this sort of punishment was ineffective against a girl who could be relied upon to repeat the offence that had led to it, often within 24 hours. There were times when he roared at her and sent her to her room. There were others when he and his wife put their heads in their hands and wept — but never when they were together.

It was difficult to imagine what the family relationship might once have been like. Certainly Mr Hudson had always been Mr Hudson and, as such, extremely rigid in his ideas, uncomprehendingly unaware of other people's feelings and acutely conscious of his public image. The managing director of his firm was a magistrate, and in his eyes the ultimate disgrace would be to have to appear in the Juvenile Court with Jane and find his boss sitting on the Bench. Mrs Hudson seemed dominated by her husband; she would doubtless be a loving, conscientious mother, thought the year tutor, but quite unable to get on the same wavelength as an independent-minded youngster.

Jane herself seemed impervious to reason, punishment or persuasion. It was as if she had enveloped herself in a hard, impenetrable shell which defied any form of attack. There was also something calculatingly provocative in her behaviour, with no trace of the frightened defiance seen in so many aggressive, frightened children and adolescents.

Jane had been referred to the consultant child psychiatrist and to an educational psychologist, much to her father's embarrassment. Neither had been able to make any helpful suggestions. "Possibly psychopathic personality", said the psychiatrist's report. The psychologist had recommended a place in the authority's centre for disruptive secondary school pupils but there were no vacancies at the time. It was thought to be only a matter of time before she committed a serious offence, found herself in the Juvenile Court and was placed in care.

She had so far steered clear of serious trouble with the police, though her insolent manner had exasperated the officer who brought her home after finding her loitering suspiciously outside a shop at 1 a.m., almost as much as it embarrassed and infuriated her father. With no special school place possible, the authority still had to provide her with some sort of education following her suspension from school. In the absence of anything better they arranged for a teacher from the home tuition service to see her at home two mornings a week.

Mrs Cryer was an unflappable, overweight lady approaching retirement, who had applied to the home tuition service in order to work with boys or girls who had broken down at school. Her offer had been accepted eagerly; most applicants specifically said that they did not want responsibility for this sort of child.

Mrs Cryer was undismayed by Jane's record. She was not even put out by Jane's opening gambit, "You can cry at me as much as you like, but if I don't feel like working I won't work, and if I don't feel like turning up I won't turn up!"

"No, love", said Mrs Cryer equably. "Now about this maths. . . ." "And I

125

don't like being called love", snapped Jane. "No, love", said Mrs Cryer. Jane started to reply, saw the glint of amusement in her teacher's eye and decided to co-operate — for the time being.

Yet Mrs Cryer was more puzzled than she was willing to admit by the hardness of Jane's shell, the calculating defiance and provocation. She penetrated the shell accidentally. The whole family was having coffee, before the parents went out together, leaving Jane to complete her morning's work with Mrs Cryer. (This was strictly against the authority's regulations, which insisted that a parent should be in the house throughout the session, but Mrs Cryer had always taken the view that regulations made good guides but bad masters.) Mrs Hudson said something which reminded Mrs Cryer of her grandmother. "My grandmother always used to say that", she remarked. "Have you got a grandmother, Jane?" At once the atmosphere seemed to have changed; Mrs Hudson was suddenly busy drying a tea cup; Mr Hudson was reading the paper and Jane was picking at a spot on her hand. "Er, no, she died five years ago", said Mr Hudson, and got up to go out with his wife, leaving his coffee half finished.

Mrs Cryer finished her coffee in silence, then leant back in her chair and said, "Jane, love, am I right in thinking that you remember your gran rather well?" All of a sudden, the shell fell away and there was a tearful, frightened child next to her. "Yes", was the answer. "And your grandfather?" "Yes." "Can you tell me about them?" "They both died, first my grandad when I was nine, and then my gran when I was eleven, just after I started at Henry Beardsley." There were tears now, but a note of angry defiance that Mrs Cryer had never heard from Jane before.

"Can you tell me about them?" she asked. "They were like my mum and dad to me. I thought of them as my mum and dad and when they died I thought . . . I thought that I'd have to look after myself, and I have too." Mrs Cryer said slowly, "I think I understand, when your grandma died you felt . . ."

"Angry", said Jane. "I didn't cry and they said I didn't care, but that just showed me they couldn't understand and that I had to look after myself." "Is this the first time you've cried about them?" asked the teacher. "No, but it's the first time I've let anyone see me", answered Jane.

With a sudden certainty Mrs Cryer saw that Jane, at the age of eleven, and probably earlier, had written her parents off as parents. Ever since, she had been using all her emotional energy to fill the gap left by her grandparents' death — or rather, to prevent it from being filled. As they continued talking, she realised that Jane had felt able to cope with her loneliness, anger and despair only by challenging the world to do its worst and proving to the world that she could take anything it threw at her without being hurt. "And was there no other way, no one else you could have come to trust?" asked Mrs Cryer gently. There was a long pause. "There might have been", said Jane, "but I couldn't see it, and I get too many kicks out of what I do to change now. You remember telling me last week that prison was the end of the road? Well, that's right, and when I go there I'll be able to cope with that too."

Mrs Cryer felt more helpless than at any time since she started home teaching, five years earlier. She realised that parents and school had failed to understand

126

Jane's feelings at the time when that was most needed. Now Jane had made her own decision and it was too late to change.

Questions

1 Do you think the school was correct in considering that the incident for which Jane was suspended would not, on its own, have been serious enough to warrant suspension?

2 If the incident *had* occurred in isolation, what steps could the school have taken, short of suspension, to impress on Jane and her parents the seriousness of the offence? What punishment would have been appropriate? What other investigations might have been appropriate?

3 Do you agree with the year tutor's implied belief that a difficult girl is more difficult than a difficult boy? How far is this a reflection of society's different expectations of boys and girls?

4 Mr and Mrs Hudson are both said to have wept about Jane's problems — but never when they were together. What does this tell you about communication within the family? How might a social worker try to improve this?

5 Do you think Mr Hudson is genuinely concerned about Jane? Could concern for his public image and love of his daughter be reconciled?

6 Do you think Mrs Cryer's reply to Jane's opening gambit was appropriate? Could that sort of reply be appropriate in an ordinary school classroom?

7 What are the reasons for the authority insisting that a parent be present throughout the home tuition session?

8 Do you think Mrs Cryer read too much into the change of mood when she asked about Jane's grandparents?

9 Can you think of incidents when you have accidentally asked children or parents questions that have led to a subtle increase in tension?

10 How could the school have recognised the reasons for Jane's disturbed behaviour when it started? Which teacher should have been responsible for its initial investigation?

11 Do you accept Mrs Cryer's conclusion that Jane had written off her parents as parents and was now determined to be entirely self-sufficient?

12 Do you accept that Jane now gets too many "kicks" from her own behaviour to have any motivation to change?

13 How could Jane and her parents have been helped if the reason for her disturbance had been recognised soon after the time of her grandmother's death?

14 Is there any way she could be helped now?

15 Is there any way her parents could be helped now?

Oakden Grammar School

Main themes

1 Provision for problem pupils will not, on its own, raise a school's standards.
2 A non-teaching counsellor may be able to help certain children and offer support or advice to staff; she will not be able to do anything about those aspects of a school's organisation and relationships which precipitate the problems of the children she counsels.

Oakden Grammar School had served its market town of some 30,000 inhabitants since the last century. Its present status as a selective grammar school was derived from the 1944 Education Act and had remained unaltered in spite of pressure from the Labour minority on the County Council and a Labour Government, to merge into the comprehensive system.

Pupils continued to be selected on the basis of the 11+ exam, which the head staunchly defended on educational and scientific grounds, until an educational psychologist expressed mild surprise that he should be so enamoured with these psychologist-devised tests, yet so critical of everything else that psychologists said and did. Oakden Grammar had room for 350 pupils, about 10 per cent of the total annual intake of eleven-year-olds into the authority's schools.

The children were streamed by ability from the word go. Streaming was based on 11+ results and reports from primary school head teachers. At the end of their first term the children took exams and most years roughly 20 per cent of the intake were moved up or down a form. At the end of their third year they had to decide whether to concentrate on science subjects or languages and the arts, though all pupils took maths, French and English language at "O" level. Apart from setting in maths and French, all lessons were form taught.

The results were mixed. The best measure – and the head's only measure – was external examinations. Over half the top form obtained at least five "O" levels each year, and a quarter of these went on to pass at least two "A" levels. Each year the school obtained an acceptable number of university places, including one or two at Oxford and Cambridge. The lowest of the three streamed forms obtained much less satisfactory results. They were traditionally known as the Pond, since their form teacher's classroom overlooked a muddy pond in the school grounds. The symbolism, however, was both intended and recognised by pupils and teachers alike. This class was expected to average one or two "O" levels, though the occasional boy or girl surprised everyone and reached the dizzy heights of four or five (and a rather large number surprised no one by failing everything).

Pastoral care had not been heard of at Oakden – or to be fairer and more accurate, it had been heard of as something that existed to modify the anarchy of the comprehensive system. "We've no room here for teachers who can't teach", Basil Kidson, the headmaster, used to say. "If they can't make the grade as teachers, I'm not going to help them find an alternative career ladder by inventing children with problems!"

He was in fact being less than fair to many of his staff. If pastoral care means knowing the children and their families, being alert to any fall-off in educational performance or change of mood, encouraging a wide range of out-of-school interests, and so on, then the "A" stream pupils at Oakden received a high quality of pastoral care. The "B" stream received a lower, but still acceptable quality, while the "C" stream was left to look after itself.

Basil Kidson's outspoken criticism of the vagaries of the allegedly "pupil-centred" comprehensive system had, however, taken two jolts recently. The first came when the heads of three of the local secondary modern schools published their examination results and showed beyond any reasonable doubt that their most successful 10 per cent of pupils were obtaining better "O" level results than the bottom stream at Oakden; indeed their results were nearly as good as his second stream. By combining all the results he was still safely ahead, but he realised with alarm that if any of the Labour councillors on his board of governors had the wit to demand a breakdown of the figures by stream he would look extremely stupid. To make matters worse, one or two of his own staff just might tip them off.

The other thing that had recently jolted his complacence was closer to home. His oldest daughter was reaching adolescence and he found himself in the middle of the traumas which he so often told parents of his pupils not to put up with. The result was that he either had to change his own attitudes, or turn his home into a battle ground. Being a sensible sort of man, he decided – or perhaps his wife and daughter decided for him – to look after his blood pressure by taking the peaceful way out.

Now there was no earthly reason why the change from benevolent despotism to benevolent tolerance at home should have been matched by a similar change at school. Yet this undoubtedly happened. The staff suddenly found themselves being urged to look for reasons for bad work or poor behaviour, even in the Pond. Life had been much easier when these children could simply be punished!

The point was that it never occurred to Basil Kidson that his poor exam results, compared with the politically-motivated secondary moderns, were caused by poor teaching or by any inherent faults in the school organisation. All the same, he did feel that many of his pupils needed a sympathetic ear from time to time, and this sympathetic ear might in some undefined way help them to settle down and eventually pass their exams. Gradually, the idea of appointing a counsellor to the school staff took shape. Some pupils, he reasoned, needed a firm, no-nonsense approach, while others would respond better to a more understanding, sympathetic approach from someone who was independent of the teaching staff, and hence removed from the academic pressures.

Basil Kidson could not have explained how a counsellor might help a child settle, nor why the three secondary modern schools seemed to be achieving good results without a counsellor's services. Nevertheless, he felt, and his staff agreed, that the experiment was worthwhile.

The lady appointed was a trained psychiatric social worker who had been out of work following her arrival in the area six months earlier when her husband took up a new job. She was middle aged, (old, said most of her customers) with a comforting, relaxed manner. Children might see her in one of two ways. They could be sent by their class teacher or by the head, or they could come on their own initiative. She was available to any youngster throughout the lunch hour, but would see pupils referred by teachers at other times. She was paid for five sessions a week, but her working hours were flexible.

On one thing the head and she had reached agreement with an ease that initially surprised her. Whether pupils referred themselves or were referred, they would see her in absolute confidence, and would know that nothing they said would go back to their teachers. The question of parents was more difficult; Basil Kidson was a little worried about parents objecting to their children being seen by the school counsellor without their consent. Mrs Perkins, herself, though, saw less of a problem. "Just put a note in your next letter to parents to say that you've appointed a counsellor to help children who seem to be having difficulty at school. Put it with the bit about other new staff and no one will turn a hair!" She was right. Nevertheless, she did meet parents, since many of the pupils asked her to see them.

At first, both teachers and pupils were a bit slow to accept the new service, but after six months Mrs Perkins had established herself as part of the school while at the same time independent of it. Every lunchtime there was a steady trickle of boys or girls making appointments to see her. Occasionally a teacher would approach her for advice about how to help a child. In these cases she would politely arrange to see the teacher later, and meanwhile ascertain whether the child had any objection to her talking to him. More often, she took the initiative herself, though only with the child's permission and had a quiet word with a teacher about the problems a child was facing, or the approach to which she thought he might respond.

A year after her appointment, Basil Kidson was delighted with the success of the experiment. Mrs Perkins' presence was clearly filling a need; informal comments from parents as well as pupils were highly complimentary. Three years later, though, he was upset to note that his exam results were no better; if anything they were worse compared with those of the top 10 per cent of the local secondary moderns. He mentioned his disappointment to Mrs Perkins. She was astonished, "Oh, but my goodness, you can't expect *me* to do anything about *that*!" she exclaimed. "That's nothing to do with me – it's to do with the teaching and organisation of the school – your department entirely!"

130

Questions

1 Can you comment on the streaming policy at Oakden Grammar School? How does it differ from the setting policy at many comprehensive schools?

2 How do you rate the exam results of the "A", "B" and "C" streams?

3 How far are the poor results of the "C" stream children a consequence of the school's streaming policy? Can you think of children from schools in which you have taught, who have lived down to their teachers' expectations in this way?

4 Do you agree with the description of pastoral care — "being alert to fall-off in educational performance or changes of mood, encouraging a wide range of out-of-school interests, and so on"? If so, do you agree that the most able children at comprehensive or primary schools in which you have taught receive an adequate quality of pastoral care?

5 Why do you think the secondary modern school heads publicised their exam results?

6 The head's attitude towards his pupils changed as his own daughter grew up. Have your own attitudes towards teaching changed as a result of having children of your own?

7 Is the head's distinction between pupils who need "a firm, no-nonsense approach" and pupils who "respond better to a more understanding, sympathetic approach" a valid one? Do the two groups overlap?

8 What are the arguments for and against a counsellor who is independent of the staff and thus removed from academic pressures? What are the arguments in favour of appointing someone who is not a teacher?

9 Do you agree with Mrs Perkins' view that her interviews with children should be absolutely confidential? What sort of problems might result from this view?

10 Is it right that a counsellor should be able to see children without their parents' consent?

11 Is Mrs Perkins right to insist that educational standards were nothing to do with her — in fact the head's department entirely?

Tony

Main themes

1 Frequent accidents should not be regarded as just an unfortunate coincidence.

2 As well as being the result of stress, accidents can sometimes help to reduce it.

"Mrs P., is it just bad luck whan a boy keeps injuring his hand or can there be some psychological explanation?" Tony Rankin's class teacher seemed half concerned, half amused, as he sat in Mrs Perkins' office at the end of afternoon school. "This is the third time this year that he's had to go to hospital. The first was a hair-line fracture and he had his arm in plaster for one month and could not write for another; the second was a cut that needed three stitches and now he's sprained his wrist and got the arm in a sling. It really isn't helping his work!"

"Sounds a bit painful, too!" murmured Mrs Perkins. "Can you tell me more about him?"

Tony, it appeared, was an athletic, well-built thirteen-year-old in his second year at Oakden Grammar. At the end of his first term he had been placed in the "A" stream, largely on the strength of glowing reports from his primary school and an outstanding 11 + score. He had done moderately well throughout his first year at the school, but had not really fulfilled the early expectations. In his second year the series of accidents had virtually put a stop to his written work and his general alertness and interest in lessons had definitely deteriorated. There was even talk of moving him down to the "B" stream, a most unusual move at Oakden. "How did the accidents happen?" asked Mrs Perkins. They all had good explanations; he had fallen over a hurdle, cut his hand on a broken pane of glass while larking about with a friend, and twisted his wrist while weight-lifting. "His father's most co-operative with the school, and he's going absolutely spare about it", continued the class teacher. Mrs Perkins asked for more information about the family. Father was a successful lawyer, mother a part-time nurse; Tony was the only boy but had three younger sisters, ranging in age from ten to one and a half. At home, according to his father on open night, he was helpful to his parents and nice to his younger sisters. "Sounds a bit too good to be true, doesn't he?" said Mrs Perkins, as much to herself as to Tony's class teacher. "Tell him that if he comes to see me tomorrow morning during assembly I'll be glad to have a word with him."

The following morning Tony had an air of injured innocence. "I've been told to come and see you by Mr Smith", he explained, "but I'm afraid I really don't know why!" Faced with this sort of introduction, Mrs Perkins tended to become a disciple of Carl Rogers. "Well, Tony, why do you think he might have asked you to come?" Tony shrugged his shoulders with a grin and supposed that his work hadn't been up to much lately because of all his accidents. "Not up to much because of all your accidents?" asked Mrs Perkins. Tony gave her an elaborate description of each one. "So your work hasn't been up to much?" Mrs Perkins commented mildly. Tony agreed that not being able to write except with your left hand did make it difficult to do essays and translations, especially when you are not ambidextrous or left-handed. "And it's affected the rest of your work, too?" Mrs Perkins' remark was as much a comment as a question. Tony looked a bit baffled, then said, "Well, what else is there?" Mrs Perkins supposed that she was out of date, but when she was at school she had to answer questions, and learn things during the lesson. "Yes", said Tony, "that still happens here." He added rather quickly. "Anyway, what is all this about?"

Mrs Perkins explained patiently that sometimes accidents happened at times when people had something on their mind, but if you were the person having the accident it was often difficult to know whether this was the case or not. Tony shrugged his shoulders. "Well I reckon I know!" he said. Mrs Perkins smiled, said she would be glad to see him at the same time the next day if he cared to come, and started to look at a book in front of her.

The next day it was not Tony who turned up but his father. "Tony gave me some garbled account of an interview with you", he explained, "so I thought I'd better come along and find out what it's all about." Mrs Perkins pulled a chair up for Mr Rankin and asked him what he thought about his son's work this year. Mr Rankin admitted to being very worried, and when Mrs Perkins pursued the matter he had to admit that Tony's general interest in school work and out-of-school activities had gone down-hill too. "But surely that's the result of struggling with his left hand all the time; it's enough to discourage anyone", he exclaimed.

"Yes, certainly, but three accidents to the same hand in such a short space of time is quite a coincidence", Mrs Perkins insisted patiently, "and it's funny how often this sort of coincidence just happens to come at a time when the child is developing – or changing – in other ways too. Have you, or your wife, for example noticed any changes or developments in his behaviour at home?" Mr Rankin thought for a moment then said that Tony had been getting on much better with his younger sisters since he had been at Oakden, but he could not think of any other recent changes. At primary school they had fought "like cats and dogs", and there had been one incident shortly before the baby was born when Mr Rankin had taken his slipper to Tony for hitting his youngest sister. This had all changed, though, after the birth of the baby, with whom Tony was marvellous. "Which was quite a relief as we were naturally concerned that he should settle well here and didn't want him upset by quarrels and arguments with his sisters at home", Mr Rankin concluded.

"Mr Rankin, have you ever thought of the possibility that the hardest people to talk to about something important are the people you are closest to, the people you love most?" For a moment Mr Rankin's composure slipped. No, he admitted, he hadn't thought of that, but he supposed it might sometimes be true. "In which case", said Mrs Perkins, getting up to conclude the interview, "I'd like your permission to see Tony two more times, and then if you both agree I'd like a chance to discuss with you, Tony and your wife whether that may be true for him." As he found himself in the corridor, Mr Rankin felt for a moment as if he had been discharged from the witness box.

Summoned from his classroom just before afternoon school, Tony looked less pleased and less confident as he entered Mrs Perkins' office. "Thank you so much for arranging for your father to come and see me, Tony", Mrs Perkins began placidly. "It was very kind of you. We arranged that I would see you twice more, and then if you agree, I might have a talk with you and your parents together." Tony's mouth dropped open in surprise. "You see", continued Mrs Perkins, "when you feel upset, or angry, or frightened about something, the people you're closest to, like your mum and dad, are the people it's hardest to tell. And I can't help wondering, Tony, whether, deep down, you've been very worried ever since you came here about whether you can do as well at school as your father expects you to?"

Tony's confidence slipped. He was looking hard at Mrs Perkins, "almost as if I were a ghost", she remarked later. Slowly he nodded his head. "How has this made you feel", Mrs Perkins went on. After another long pause, Tony replied, "That I can't do it — and mad at him, too."

Mrs Perkins spent the rest of the session reassuring Tony in simple terms that other children were under similar pressure, and that with a bit of help, he and his father together would be able to sort out what he could hope to do and what he couldn't. The next day she tackled Tony on a different subject. "Tony, yesterday we talked about your father and what you think he expects of you at school. Today I'd like your help with something else. You must tell me if I'm wrong, but I have the feeling that perhaps there's something else, at home, that you've been keeping to yourself for a year or two now." Again, the slow nod of agreement. "To do with your mum?" Tony shook his head. "Your oldest sister?" He shook his head with less confidence. "Your baby sister?" Tony nodded.

"Would it be very wrong to feel angry about a new baby arriving?" asked the counsellor patiently. Again, Tony nodded slowly. "But you do?" He nodded again, reluctantly. Mrs Perkins grinned suddenly, "Nasty, noisy, smelly things, taking up everyone's time and getting cooed over, don't you agree?" For the first time, Tony laughed. "Listen", Mrs Perkins went on, "whatever you've been thinking about your baby sister, that's just what lots of other boys and girls feel about their baby brothers and sisters. For goodness sake stop being so nice to her — she's done nothing to deserve it! Mind you, I'm not saying go and thump her when she cries or you'll get thumped yourself by your dad, and quite right too. All I mean is that you should live your own life and let her live hers."

At her meeting with the whole family the following week Mrs Perkins explained in simple terms how Tony felt under pressure at school, and how he over-compensated for his perfectly normal feelings of jealousy towards his sister. She urged the Rankins not to encourage Tony to be excessively attentive to his baby sister; conversely, his own hobbies and interests should be encouraged. Mrs Rankin said, "I can understand everything you've said so far, and we'll certainly think about it; what I don't see though, is how this has led to all his accidents." Mrs Perkins smiled. "If you really want to know what I think, you can come and see me again when Tony's left school, but if you do what we've agreed today I don't think he will have any more. Just to make sure that we are on the right lines though, could we all meet again in a month's time, and meanwhile I'll be glad to see Tony at any time, if he wants to come and see me."

Questions

1 Can you think of any "accident-prone" children from your own teaching experience? What investigations were carried out with these children?

2 The family had four children, the youngest only one and a half. Father was a successful lawyer and mother a part-time nurse. What possibilities would this information lead you to bear in mind about family attitudes, relationships and pressures in investigating possible reasons for Tony's accidents?

3 What are the main features of Rogerian therapy?

4 As a counsellor, or year tutor, how would you have handled the first interview with Tony? Do you think Mrs Perkins handled it correctly? Could you have tried to find out more at this stage?

5 Is there any similarity between Tony and his father in their initial reactions towards Mrs Perkins? Can you think of examples from your own experience when parents and children use the same strategies to insulate themselves from unpleasant or emotionally threatening thoughts or experiences?

6 Mrs Perkins concluded her first interview with Tony's father rather abruptly. Why? What two pieces of information about Tony had she inferred from what Mr Rankin had told her? Might it have been profitable to have inquired further about them at this stage?

7 Why do you think Tony looked less pleased and less confident at the start of his second interview with Mrs Perkins? What were his likely motives in getting his father to see her?

3 Do you think Mrs Perkins' questioning of Tony was too direct? Did she make it too easy for him to agree with her own ideas about the pressures he was experiencing?

9 Why did Mrs Perkins urge the Rankins not to encourage Tony to be too attentive towards his baby sister?

10 Can you think of any children who have over-compensated for feelings of guilt or hostility towards a younger sibling by becoming excessively friendly towards them? How might Tony's accidents be related to this?

11 How might Tony's accidents have reduced his anxiety about his father's unreasonably high academic expectations?

Grove Bank Comprehensive School

Main themes

1 Severe behaviour problems may be rare or unknown, even in a school serving difficult areas, but it does not follow that the school will be having equal success in catering for its withdrawn, socially inadequate children.

2 Providing the stability of a small class with only one or two teachers, along primary school class teacher lines, will not be adequate unless the children's activities are consciously geared towards their integration into the mainstream of the school.

Tim Ryder, the head of Grove Bank Comprehensive, felt quite pleased with himself as he drove back from the meeting of the authority's secondary school heads. The main item on the agenda had been the perennial topic of disruptive children, and although Grove Bank had one of the poorest catchment areas he had been pleased to note that most of his colleagues were a good deal more worried about the problem than he was himself.

Of course, the school did have its fair share of children he could quite happily manage without, and parental support was limited to say the least. Yet when he had looked through the punishment book before coming to the meeting, he had merely confirmed his impression. Only three girls had been caned in the previous year, and they were only punished for gross insolence to a student teacher in the lunch hour. Corporal punishment was used more for boys, but never for anything as desperate as the threats of physical violence or actual assaults that seemed to be preoccupying one or two other head teachers. The usual offences were truancy, repeated lateness, acts of petty thoughtlessness that could be called vandalism if you wanted to be dramatic. Better still, only two children had been excluded from school in the last eighteen months, and both of them had returned to the fold within a fortnight.

"I can't think what these other schools are doing to their kids to get them to behave like this", he said in the staff room later that day. "Honestly, there were some hair-raising accounts of things we just don't have here. Mind you, I suppose I would have searched my memory and joined in myself if I'd thought there was the slightest chance of the authority doing what they wanted."

"And what was that?" asked the head of the science faculty with interest.

"Oh, open another disruptives unit, or at least give them an additional teacher to open one themselves", answered Tim Ryder with a laugh.

Tim Ryder was not actively opposed to the idea of a behavioural unit for his school, and thought that the authority probably did need some sort of centre for pupils who wouldn't fit into other ordinary schools. He was too much of a pragmatist to have well-defined views against units as did the head and deputy at Greenfield Comprehensive School in a neighbouring authority. He would undoubtedly have dismissed them as "philosopher kings". He simply took the view that his system was working well and there was no need for change.

The visiting psychologist had every reason to agree that the system − or this part of it − was working well. Grove Bank was the only secondary school he visited which did not put him in a bound-to-fail situation by referring to him a steady stream of disruptive, disaffected pupils for whom he had nothing helpful to offer. Two things interested him, though; first how Grove Bank apparently succeeded in preventing disruptive confrontations with the potentially difficult pupils that must exist; and second, whether he and the school could do anything extra to help its exceptionaly large number of rather dull, socially inadequate children who attended erratically and seemed thoroughly out of their depth when they did attend. To be strictly honest, the psychologist had no idea whether Grove Bank did really have an exceptionally high number of these children; he just knew that they referred more than other schools. The attendance problem was less often truancy than absence condoned by parents, sometimes in the form of unnecessarily prolonged illness, but it was not hard to see why the children opted out in the first place when they were so out of their depth academically.

The reason for Grove Bank's success in preventing disruptive behaviour was not one that lent itself to favourable quotation by the authority's liberal (some heads said trendy) advisers and psychologists. The prevailing wisdom held that mixed-ability grouping was associated with better standards, yet Grove Bank had two broad ability bands with setting in each band.

Rather, the reason seemed to lie in the number of very experienced, very strong, very senior staff who had been in the school for at least ten years and in one case nearly forty. These teachers were all strong disciplinarians and they all backed up their junior colleagues. Discipline was not maintained through frequent corporal punishment; as we have seen, this was used, but less frequently than in neighbouring schools. It was maintained because the school was stable at the top and this stability filtered down into the classroom.

In fact, there was another side to the picture of stability at the top. This was that the academic standards had not progressed much since the school's secondary modern days. "We've got such stability that the curriculum has stagnated in at least three crucial areas", a young graduate on the staff had remarked to the maths adviser as they had a drink after an evening course. Tim Ryder recognised this, though he would not have put it in such strong terms, but regarded it as the price to pay for a generally happy and contented atmosphere in the school. In any case, he had only another six years before retirement and thought he was too old for anything radical.

The questions of poor attendance and inadequate children who seemed unable to cope with ordinary school life were, however, less easy to explain. Tim Ryder accepted the educational psychologist's suggestion that these were both genuine problems which needed further examination. They agreed that the deputy head, heads of two of the school's four pastoral care house groups, and the psychologist would look at the question together and then discuss it with him.

They started with a list of the nine poor attenders who had been referred to the psychologist over the last two years, and added to this four other children who attended well, yet seemed hopelessly out of their depth socially, in spite of having adequate educational attainments. The heads of house then went through their own house lists, and asked their two colleagues to do likewise, in an attempt to identify other similar children who had not actually been referred to the psychological service. At the end of this exercise they had a combined list of 25 children.

They then started to identify the common features in these pupils. This was more difficult than it seemed. Each child was known well by one teacher, but not generally by more than one. As a result there were a lot of anecdotes but few conclusions. Gradually, though, a reasonably consistent picture emerged. The children covered the whole age range, but the majority were in their first two or three years at the school, and in all cases the problem had started in the child's first year. Over three-quarters were educationally retarded, though not always so retarded as to be placed in the remedial department.

About half seemed to have no friends at school. When these children truanted they tended to stay on their own, generally fairly close to were they lived. Often their mothers would give up the unequal struggle to get them to attend. The other half did have friends, "But their friends are as unsuitable for them as they are for their friends", the deputy head remarked. These pupils truanted frequently, and committed offences in each other's company both in and out of school.

"So it looks as if we are identifying a small, but time-consuming group of children with whom we are not having much success at the moment", the deputy concluded their review. "I think it would be fair to say", he went on, "that we've been making full use of the psychological and education welfare services, and that your help", he turned to the psychologist, "has given us a much better idea of the nature of this problem; but I also think it's fair to say that you haven't been able to cure it for us. When I look at the children and families concerned, I don't see how you possibly could. What we need to do now is think what we can do about it ourselves, using whatever help and advice is available from the support services."

The psychologist heaved a brief sigh of relief. He had been afraid for a moment that the deputy was going to refer more children to him, in which case he would have had to point out the continuing poor attendance of the children who *had* been referred!

"What these children need is someone to take a personal interest in them the whole time they are in school", one of the heads of house argued, "rather like the primary school class teacher system, but in a much smaller class." This, though, was an over-simplification for two reasons. The first reason was that the children did not just need more consistent contact with a stable adult than could be provided in the normal time-table in which each child was taught by ten or eleven teachers a week. They also needed to learn how to cope with the day-to-day demands of social life in a large school. What this boiled down to was building up their confidence in getting on with other children. The second reason was that the children probaby did not need someone to look after them the whole time; what they needed was a secure base from which to integrate themselves gradually into ordinary lessons and out-of-school activities.

Coming to these conclusions took the group a long time, but when they eventually met Tim Ryder to discuss their ideas, they had a well-prepared case for a "half-way house" to cater for children who were at present failing to cope with the system. The half-way house would consist of a small group. It would not admit pupils who had been seriously disruptive in school. The majority of children would be admitted following a period of truancy or school refusal, and the class would aim to ease their path back into school. A few other pupils would also be admitted who seemed unhappy or out of their depth socially in the school, even though they might not have presented any attendance problem.

"Obviously, we haven't thought out the details, headmaster", explained a head of house, "but we thought we ought to discuss our preliminary ideas with you at this stage, so that you could decide whether we should go ahead."

Questions

1 Do you agree that the record of sanctions used at Grove Bank School in the last year and a half is a creditable one?

2 The head seems to think some other schools were themselves contributing towards their pupils' bad behaviour. How might this happen?

3 Can you think of instances from your own experience where educational psychologists have been "put in a bound-to-fail situation"? Is referral sometimes motivated by the need to share anxiety (or even to "pass the buck") rather than by any realistic appraisal of the good it will do? Is this justified? Is the aim of referral: (i) to secure treatment for the child, or (ii) to discuss his management and education with an independent outsider?

4 The psychologist did not seem to know how Grove Bank succeeded in preventing confrontations with its difficult pupils. Have you any ideas?

5 Do you agree with the reasons given for the school's success in containing its potentially disruptive pupils? What other explanations are there?

6 In a school of around 1,000 pupils, does the list of 25 children with problems of poor attendance and/or of social inadequacy seem excessive?

7 Would you have wished membership of the study group to be expanded to include form tutors, heads of departments and remedial teachers?

8 Do you accept the validity of the deputy head's assessment that support services cannot deal with the problem, only support the teachers in their attempts to deal with it themselves?

9 Do you agree that it was an oversimplification to say that the children needed someone to take a personal interest in them the whole time they were in school?

10 How do you *teach* withdrawn, socially inadequate children to cope with the day-to-day demands of a large school? How do you teach them to have greater confidence in themselves?

11 Prepare a detailed plan for the "half-way house" proposed to Tim Ryder.

Joanne

Main themes

1 As they start to feel more sure of themselves, insecure children often show behaviour problems which are more disruptive than the problems which originally caused concern.

2 Treating behaviour problems and good teaching are not separate skills. The principles of good teaching apply as much in the treatment of emotional or behavioural problems as in the teaching of any academic subject.

Joanne was one of the first children referred to the small group that opened in Grove Bank School the following year. She seemed just the sort of girl it was intended for. In school she had only one friend, another placid girl whom teachers could easily overlook. She was never an active nuisance, but she nevertheless had enormous nuisance value; she was always losing her time-table, arriving late to lessons, forgetting her PE kit, losing, or more probably, not doing, her homework.

Her attendance had always been irregular and at the start of her second year at Grove Bank School it became worse. At first the school thought her parents were covering up for her; in the past colds and 'flu had dragged on a suspiciously long time. Eventually, though, the education welfare officer (e.w.o.) had proved that she was truanting, though she never strayed far from the high-rise flat where she lived, and she was always alone. "A bit worrying, you know, a twelve-year-old girl who's as suggestible as Joanne hanging around on her own all day in an area like that", he said to Joanne's head of house.

Her educational attainments were poor. The primary school report said this was partly due to family circumstances, and partly due to her having missed over a year's schooling at the age of ten with a broken leg. "Of course, the authority arranged home tuition when they realised she would be at home for so long", explained the head on the phone, "but you see they hadn't any spare teachers until her last month at home, so it was all a bit of a waste of time."

Joanne was the third of four children, and her family circumstances were not favourable. Her mother lived on social security and the father's whereabouts had been unknown since he deserted the family two years earlier, after years of friction. Nevertheless, the children were obviously fed and clothed well, (though Grove Bank teachers had long given up the unequal struggle of persuading any of the Wests to wear full school uniform) and the home was untidy but certainly not dirty. The older children had attended school well enough to keep the e.w.o. away from the family door more than once a month. Her brother had left school the previous summer with two CSEs at grade 3, while her sister was now in her final year.

Mrs West had agreed to Joanne being placed in the unit without hesitation. "Anything you say, dear!" she told the head of house and Roy Powell, head of the unit. "I just want to get her settled." It seemed to the two teachers that Mrs West really did want to get Joanne settled, but that she didn't expect to do much about it herself. At home Joanne was apparently "a bit of a devil, you know" but the cheerful glint in Mrs West's eye as she said it made clear that she did not think there was anything to worry too much about.

The plan was that Joanne should attend the unit full-time to start with. It was then hoped to persuade her to attend her normal class for registration, and gradually to return to ordinary lessons. Her first day with Roy Powell in the unit was in fact her first day back in school for nearly a month. She was the soul of co-operation and helpfulness − "Sickening really", Roy remarked in the staff room to the head of house, "I'm not sure I wouldn't have preferred her to swear at me, I'd have been more convinced it was genuine!"

Joanne's co-operation and helpfulness continued for the next week. Roy wasn't quite sure if the change came because the novelty had worn off, or because he had started to require more work from her, or even because she thought it time to see whether he could cope with the other side of her personality. In any event, Joanne's helpfulness faded and then disappeared altogether. She didn't become openly aggressive or even defiant; she simply carried out the basic minimum of work and put no effort into the little work she did produce. What was probably worse, she either ignored the other four children in the unit altogether or else argued with them. For their part, they ignored her most of the time but occasionally provoked her into retaliation by bumping into her "accidentally" or by calling her Joanne North, South, East and West.

Roy realised that he was seeing a more extreme form of the behaviour which had led to Joanne's referral to the unit in the first place, with the notable exception that she was still attending regularly. "Damn it, I thought the idea was to make them better, not worse!" the head of house said good humouredly in the staff room when Roy told him about Joanne's lack of progress. "It's OK for you to be cheerful, you haven't got the ruddy girl all day", Roy snapped back, "and don't tell me I applied for the job!"

At about this time Roy decided to involve the children more closely in recording their own progress. At the beginning of each day he drew up a programme of activities for each child to complete. The activities ranged from formal work assignments to group activities which involved games and co-operative group work on a project. On a separate sheet he wrote a list of activities which each child had suggested because he enjoyed doing it and would like an opportunity to select it on completion of his work programme. The list ranged from reading comics to making coffee (previously purchased), drawing, painting, playing table tennis, and so on. The periods from 11.30−12.00 in the morning, and 3.30−4.00 in the afternoon, were set aside for the children to select their own activities, *provided* they had carried out their programme of assignments to his satisfaction. If they had not completed their morning or afternoon programme to his satisfaction they had to carry on with work he gave them in these periods.

In this way Roy thought he could give each child an incentive to make progress in the programme which he, Roy, had selected. For example, children who needed to learn to play or work co-operatively with other children might find their morning assignment included half an hour playing Scrabble or some other game. In fact, thought Roy, that might be quite a good assignment for children who couldn't cope with frustration. Similarly, pupils who had frequently been in trouble for their surly or indifferent manner to teachers might be expected to take part in role play sessions in which they practised different ways to behave in these situations.

For Joanne there was one rather obvious flaw in this scheme. She thought it was a waste of time because she didn't have anything she really wanted to do in the free-choice sessions − and as there was nothing she really wanted to do, she did not see any point in putting herself out to complete her programme of assignments.

Faced with an impasse Roy became devious. "Are you really telling me all you want to do is sit on your own and do nothing?" he snapped. Joanne said she didn't see why she should do anything. "Fine", said Roy and wrote "Nothing" in large letters on the list of activities for pupils to select in the free-choice sessions. The next day he prepared a programme of assignments that was so short that even Joanne could not fail to complete them. At 11.30 the other children chose to make coffee and read comics. These were activities they had already asked Roy to put on the list. Naturally he agreed. "But you, Joanne", he said, "have only chosen nothing, so you must now sit at your desk and do nothing!"

"I've changed my mind!" said Joanne. "Well I haven't!" said Roy. "I'll listen to changes from you and anyone else this afternoon, but not in free-choice time. Sit down, and don't let me see you reading, writing, or doing anything!" Joanne was furious − more animated than Roy had ever seen her before − but eventually she sat down and spent the half-hour glaring malevolently at Roy and the other children.

That afternoon she asked with heavy sarcasm, "Please, *sir*, are we allowed to choose other things now, or do we have to do our work first?" Roy replied lightly, "You've got three assignments, Joanne, you can take five minutes off after the first one to tell me what else you might like to do in free-choice time."

Joanne's progress was not exactly smooth after this incident, but it did seem to have broken the previous pattern of passive non-co-operation. By the end of the term she was starting to return to carefully selected lessons with the rest of her class, and by the end of the following term she was only attending the unit for two sessions a week, "just to keep in touch" as she put it herself.

The psychologist had followed Roy's experiment with interest. "I see you're applying the Premack Principle", he said appreciatively. "Oh yes", said Roy, "what's that?" "There's quite an extensive literature on it, actually", said the psychologist. "It was developed in the laboratory with rats; what it comes down to is that if you follow something unpleasant with something pleasant then the thing that was originally considered unpleasant becomes more popular. I could give you one or two journal articles on its use with children, if you like."

"No thanks", replied Roy, "I'll stick to common sense for the moment!"

Questions

1 The e.w.o. was worried about Joanne truanting on her own. Professionals often seem to be more worried about girls being in moral danger than boys. What rational justification is there for this? For example, would girls be less likely to become pregnant and boys less likely to make them pregnant if they were in care?

2 How does the Home Tuition service seem to cope with its waiting list?

3 What do you infer about relationships in the home from the account of Mrs West's interview with Roy Powell?

4 Joanne's initial behaviour was too good to be true. In what other ways might her behaviour have been expected to develop? Have you taught children who went through similar stages?

5 Do you think Roy Powell was correct in thinking Joanne's behaviour in the unit was simply a more extreme form of her previous behaviour in ordinary class?

6 What do you think about Roy Powell's decision to involve the children more closely in recording their own progress? Do you agree with his method? If not, give a detailed description of an alternative.

7 The assignments Roy Powell gave each child were selected on the basis of each child's problems. In other words he was integrating a programme to deal with their behaviour with a programme of academic work. Describe how you would do this with a difficult child you have taught yourself.

8 Do you agree with Roy's way out of his impasse with Joanne? Do you think the other children would have considered it fair? Would it have been reasonable for Roy to have backed down earlier?

9 How else might Roy Powell have broken the pattern of non-co-operation?

10 What are the principal difficulties in applying the Premack Principle in an ordinary school classroom? Why would it be easier in a primary school?

Castle Square Comprehensive School

Main themes

1 Educational decisions, for example on record keeping, can have far-reaching political implications.

2 Record-keeping systems have to recognise the parents' right to information as well as the teachers'.

3 Record-keeping systems need to be up-dated regularly in the face of changing circumstances.

"This is just *stupid*!" Kaye Hackett, first year tutor at Castle Square Comprehensive School was seething. "I'm meant to be a year tutor and I not only can't get hold of information about a child, I find that there's no way for anyone else to either!" Her irritation was understandable. She had to write a court report on a boy in her year, and knew that he had been seen by the local child guidance clinic and that his family was known to the N.S.P.C.C., though she had never seen any reports. She had also just discovered that he had a history of poor health. This last bit of information had come to her quite by accident when she heard the PE teacher say he had forgotten to find something for Paul to do during PE. It appeared that the previous Summer term, Paul and his parents had visited the school and the parents had explained that Paul would not be able to do PE because of an intestinal operation a few months earlier. The PE teacher was told and made a note in his own department's records, but no record had been put in the school's central records on each pupil.

The child guidance report was eventually traced to the deputy head's file of confidential reports, and three months later a letter from the N.S.P.C.C. to the head turned up in the school doctor's file. These were kept permanently locked as they were regarded as confidential medical information, though the school doctor would always divulge relevant information when asked specifically. "Information that a child is deaf or short-sighted is apparently too confidential for lesser mortals like teachers", groaned Kaye Hackett. "If we're not told by the parents or the primary schools – and primary schools never tell us anything – we have to guess for ourselves, and then the doctor will look in her little file to see if we are right!" Psychologists' reports went from the head to the deputy; he either filed them in his "confidential" folder or passed them to the year tutor, head of the remedial department or class teacher depending on their content. "Or your mood", said Kaye belligerently as she told him about her difficulty in writing the court report.

The reason for the muddle was not hard to see. Until the last two years, Castle Square had been a small comprehensive drawing its pupils from middle schools in comfortable, well-to-do suburbs on the outskirts of a large city. With no eleven-year-old entry, the numbers never exceeded 350, including the small sixth form; pastoral care and co-operation with external agencies had resided with the head and her deputy, both of whom had retired just before a large influx of children from two new housing estates. Not only did these children more than double the numbers in the school, they also altered the social balance.

The head and deputy met all prospective parents and personally obtained details about any medical or emotional problems. As a double check the deputy paid a social visit to his colleagues in the feeding primary schools, but this seldom resulted in additional information. The system was relaxed, informal but effective. Now, with the number swollen to 1,000, and a new head and a new deputy, it was casual, chaotic and ineffective.

Kaye's frustration was shared by Len Lister, the new deputy; he had in fact mentioned it to the head more than once, but the pressing problem of curriculum re-organisation and time-tabling in a rapidly expanding school had kept them fully stretched. In the course of their first year numbers had expanded from 390 to 700 as the housing department moved families out of inner-city demolition zones into the newly completed houses on the outskirts. Fortunately the authority had completed the additional building in time. They had also been generous with staffing; the school had started each year grossly over-staffed in anticipation of the expansion, and the pupil–teacher ratio had not quite risen to the city average by the end of the year.

At the next meeting of the school's senior management, Len Lister proposed that he should review the school's record-keeping procedures in the light of problems that had arisen recently. "Kaye Hackett tends to shoot her mouth off", he said, "but she's quite right to be concerned about it, so I'd like to bring her in as well." The head did not answer at once. He was aware that members of the Education Committee were asking critical questions about parents' lack of access to confidential records in schools. He did not want to set up something that could misfire and explode in their faces. "All right", he said at last, "but bear in mind that this is a sensitive issue politically. I'll pass you the relevant Education Committee minutes, and I think you should look at the relevant section of the Warnock Report. There's been some publicity in recent issues of *Where* too; you'd better take a look at it."

Len Lister and Kaye Hackett did their homework thoroughly. They decided to list records under two headings: (i) the school's own records and all communications between school and parents, and (ii) all communications with agencies or individuals outside the school. Each heading was then subdivided into two parts, records that could be shown at any time to parents and records that must remain confidential at all times.

"Is there any real reason", asked Kaye, "why any of our own internal records should not be available to parents on request?" There *are* things in some of my files that I would not really want parents to see, but I'm not sure that these should be kept on file anyway." Len was uncertain. He also believed that schools tended to withhold too much information but was not sure that it would help for parents to see some of the comments written, for instance, on children's daily report sheets. "I think I agree with you that some comments should not have been written", he said, "but teaching is a stressful enough job without having to ask yourself whether everything you write is fit for parents to see as well as for the senior teacher who requested it. Besides, I'm not sure what the union position is on this."

Kaye objected that parents were surely entitled to know what punishments their children had received, and for what reason. They eventually decided that the standard Education Record Card would have to be re-designed to include space for a list of the child's achievements and other incidents − "crime and punishment" said Len dryly. If a child was placed on daily report, or a note of complaint was received, the facts and outcomes could be summarised, but the actual report sheets and other notes would be confidential to the teacher to whom they were sent and should be destroyed at the end of the term.

The question of communication with outside agencies was more difficult. The primary schools' records were the first problem. Although the primary schools seemed to put virtually no information on their record cards, they expressed alarm and surprise at the idea that they should be shown to parents. "We could always ask them not to give us anything which they don't want us to show parents", said Len, "but that's a matter for the head to decide." They decided without much difficulty that all communications from the school to outside agencies should be available to parents. "This means we will have to be careful how we word some of our letters", Kaye said. "For instance when we are writing to social services about a possible case of child abuse." Len agreed but thought that as long as all letters went through him or the head the conflicting demands of openness and protection of the school's teachers could probably be reconciled.

Communications from outside agencies such as the psychological service, child guidance, education welfare, social services, and so on, had to be treated differently, though. Since these letters were generally labelled confidential the school had to regard them as such. Their decision was to keep these in Len's office unless their nature made it obviously appropriate for them to be on open access. An example was a letter from a hospital consultant to the head about some aspect of a child's physical health which would affect his performance in class. Placing a letter in the confidential file was, however, to be recorded on the new Education Record Card.

"We've spent a lot of time deciding what to record and whether parents should have access to it", said Kaye, "but we haven't thought yet about who should be responsible for keeping the records and circulating the information collected to teachers who need it." Len replied firmly that this was the year tutor's job, except in the case of letters from outside agencies which he would show the year tutor and any other teachers who needed the information before filing it. "I think the records should be kept locked in the year tutor's office", he continued. "Any teacher should have the right of access to them on request, but we should make clear that class teachers are expcted to read them."

Len and Kaye prepared a detailed paper on their deliberations. They also drafted a new Education Record Card to replace the outdated one provided by the authority. The head read it carefully then sent Len a note: "Thank you – a useful start – several problems – we will discuss it at the next management meeting."

Questions

1 Have you ever experienced the sort of communication problem that caused Kaye Hackett such irritation? How might it have been avoided?

2 The PE teacher assumed Paul was still unfit to do PE. Is there any evidence for this assumption?

3 What are the limits of the school doctor's responsibility? Is there a genuine case for restricting access to her file? How can she ensure that teachers receive any relevant information when they need it?

4 Do you think it necessary and/or practicable for a teacher to meet all prospective parents personally before their children start at a school? If so, how would you organise this in a comprehensive school?

5 What steps would you take to minimise the disturbance caused by an influx of children from a new housing estate, bearing in mind that these children would alter the social balance in the school?

6 How could the school minimise the educational difficulties arising from a sudden influx of pupils, many of whom might be in their fourth or fifth years and hence in the middle of courses leading to public examinations?

7 Have parents ever complained about lack of access to confidential files on their children at your own school? If you were the parent of an unsuccessful child would you be concerned – knowing what you do about the system?

8 What is your union's position on confidential records?

9 Design an Education Record Card on which to record: (i) a child's educational progress from term to term; (ii) all noteworthy achievements, problems, meetings with parents etc.

10 Do you agree with Len Lister that "as long as all letters (to outside agencies) went through him or the head, the conflicting demands of openness and protection of the school's teachers could probably be reconciled"?

11 How should parents be made aware of the content of communications from outside agencies?

12 Should *all* teachers have access to records kept in the year tutor's office?

13 What problems do you think the head had in mind when he read his colleagues' paper?

Diana

Main themes

1 Taking legal action against a family may reduce a teacher's frustration about a child's absence, but it won't necessarily help the child.
2 Education welfare is not confined to school attendance.

3 Removing a child from home may sometimes help the child concerned; yet it may also have the effect of creating further problems for other members of the family.

It was easy to reject one role, Hilda Hamilton the new education welfare officer (e.w.o.) for Castle Square thought to herself, but much harder to find a more acceptable one. As one of the few qualified social workers in the authority's education welfare service she was in an interesting position. Her superiors clearly expected her to branch out from the traditional e.w.o. role, but at the same time she felt they were intensely suspicious of new-fangled ideas. At her interview she had been asked what she thought about legal action in cases of poor attendance. She replied that as long as education was free and compulsory there would have to be some form of legal provision for parents and children who chose not to avail themselves of it. On the other hand, she went on, what little evidence had been published on the effects of legal action suggested that it was largely ineffective in improving attendance. Further, everything she had seen and heard about the families of poor attenders led her to believe that this was highly predictable. If the mother was depressed and the father out of work, there wasn't anything terribly constructive in asking the magistrates to add to the family's burdens by imposing a fine.

She hadn't expected to get the job, particularly after this speech, and had spent the two months between her interview and taking up her appointment wondering if she had made a big mistake. Now, six months later, she was becoming painfully aware of the conflict between her professional inclinations and the expectations of the school she served. The conflict was best illustrated by the case of Diana Beckett.

Diana was a tense eleven-year-old with a nervous, toothy smile. Hilda Hamilton had "become involved" as the jargon went, when the school asked her to investigate the possibility of a uniform grant as Diana never seemed to have the right clothing. On visiting the new semi, which the workmen had vacated only a fortnight before, she found Mrs Beckett shouting at the three-year-old daughter and Mr Beckett shouting at Mrs Beckett.

They were not pleased to see her, but mellowed when she explained why she had come. "No, love", Mrs Beckett explained, "we've tried before, but 'e's in work" — she jerked her thumb at Mr Beckett — "though you wouldn't believe it, the amount 'e brings home." "You know very well I can't bring you any more, Agnes", her husband snapped. Hilda pursued the subject patiently, pointing out that the family might be eligible for some benefits even though Mr Beckett was in work. Were they certain that his income was above the limit? At this point Mr Beckett said he had to go, leaving Hilda, slightly confused, with Mrs Beckett, who promptly burst into tears.

Gradually Hilda established what had happened. The three-year-old was her illegitimate child, and ever since his birth her husband had been threatening to leave her and take all the children. "Has he anywhere to go?" Hilda asked. Mrs Beckett was vague, but thought he might go to his mother's, who would probably have them "just for the spite of it." To make matters worse, her husband gave her only £35 a month to feed and clothe the whole family, even though he had a good job with the Council.

Hilda told the year tutor, Kaye Hackett, that there was no chance of a uniform grant, but please would she keep an eye on Diana, as the family circumstances were disturbing, to say the least. She made a mental note to look in again the following fortnight, but before she had done so, Kaye was asking her to visit again as Diana had not attended school for four days. Hilda's visit revealed that Mr Beckett had indeed left home, as his wife had feared, but without taking any of the five children with him. No one had heard of him since his disappearance two days after Hilda's first visit.

Mrs Beckett was in a distraught state and the children understandably upset. Diana was apologetic, "I'm sorry I haven't been to school, Miss, but I had to stay and help mum, you see." Hilda saw only too well. In the next three days she helped Mrs Beckett arrange for the children to receive free meals at school, and saw that she applied for various other benefits to which she was probably now entitled. The two primary school children returned to school, but not Diana.

At first Kaye Hackett had been sympathetic to the family's plight. Her sympathy became a bit strained when a week went by with no sign of Diana, a good deal more strained after a fortnight and broke altogether after a month. "You say you've been visiting twice a week," she exploded, "so for goodness sake, where is the ruddy girl?" Patiently, Hilda explained that Mrs Beckett was still in a highly emotional condition, ("Which makes it all the more important that her daughter should come to school", interrupted Kaye), and most of her visits were spent trying to persuade her not to throw in the sponge altogether. Diana was the most affected of the five children, probably because she was the oldest and her mother relied on her more than on the others. She was insisting on remaining at home with her mother. "You don't think my mum's fit to be left, Miss, do you?" she had asked Hilda once.

Hilda had to agree that Mrs Beckett probably wasn't in a fit state to be left, but on the other hand nor was Diana a fit person to be looking after her. Kaye said she thought social services ought to be involved. "I've already referred the family as an urgent case", replied Hilda. "In effect they thanked me for passing the buck and said they would put the Becketts on their waiting list."

A fortnight later Hilda thought they were turning the corner. Mrs Beckett was less depressed, more willing to take responsibility for the children. Diana, however, had not returned to school and was showing definite signs of severe school refusal — or rather of anxiety at the thought of leaving home. Hilda was about to seek help from the school medical officer with a view to getting a psychiatrist's opinion on Diana, when she found herself in serious conflict both with the school and with her own superiors in the education department's central offices. The head, at Kaye Hackett's insistence had written to the chief education officer formally requesting that legal action be taken under section I of the 1969 Children and Young Persons Act, to bring Diana before the Juvenile Court on the grounds of poor school attendance. Having listened in detail to the school's case, her superiors seemed inclined to agree.

Hilda was angry that the chief education welfare officer had not informed her of the request — with its implicit criticism of her work and judgement — before making his own inquiries at the school. She put her point of view forcibly, "If I hadn't helped Mrs Beckett, she would have broken down altogether and then all the children would have gone into care. That might have pleased certain teachers at Castle Square School, but you know as well as I do that it wouldn't have benefited the children. As it is, Mrs Beckett's picking up the pieces of her life again, two of the children are back at school and Diana's the only one we have good reason to be worried about. Taking her to court and putting her in a Children's Home might please Kaye Hackett, but I believe Diana and her mother need treatment, not punishment — which is why I've written to her GP asking him to refer her to a psychiatrist."

The chief e.w.o. looked at her thoughtfully. "All right", he said at last, "but I don't know why you didn't try the l.e.a.'s own service first. There's a very able psychologist who visits Castle Square. More to the point, are you going to be able to re-establish a working relationship with the school?"

Questions

1 What is the role of the e.w.o. at your school? What part should school attendance play in his work?

2 What are your views about legal action against poor attenders and/or their parents? Is it possible that such action might create more problems than it solves?

3 Who has the legal responsibility for ensuring that a child receives education appropriate to his age, ability and aptitude?

4 What is the statutory provision for legal action against parents over their children's poor attendance?

5 What are the current thresholds for social benefits such as free school meals, family income supplement, rate rebate and so on? Is it possible that all or any of these may be payable if a parent is in full-time employment?

6 The text says that the e.w.o. arranged for Mrs Beckett to receive benefits "in the next three days". Do the authorities in your area move that fast?

7 Could Hilda Hamilton have taken further steps to persuade the social services department to move more quickly?

8 What are the "definite signs of school refusal"? In what circumstances is it desirable to seek a psychiatrist's opinion? Is it ever necessary to seek a psychiatrist's opinion without first seeking advice from the authority's own educational psychologist?

9 Children cannot be brought before the Juvenile Court for poor attendance *per se*. How can poor attendance be used in bringing a child to court?

10 Did the e.w.o. need to write to the GP in order to refer Diana to a psychiatrist? Is there any other channel?

11 Do you agree with Hilda Hamilton's view that her superiors acted unfairly?

13 Do you agree with her defence of her decision not to seek legal action over this case?

13 What reply would you expect the chief education welfare officer to give the head teacher?

14 What action might the head have taken before writing to the office?

15 In Hilda Hamilton's place, how would you set about re-establishing a working relationship with the school's teachers?

Greenfield Comprehensive School

Main themes

1 Knowledge of a child's background is only relevant if it will help teachers to meet his needs more effectively.

2 As leaders of a pastoral team, year tutors should not see themselves primarily as trouble-shooters dealing with problem children.

At the end of his second year in teaching, both spent at Greenfield, Keith Evans was informally advised to apply for a year tutor's vacancy. The promotion, rapid to say the least, was explained by the fact that he had come into teaching after five successful years as a residential social worker, for the last two of which he had been deputy of a large boys' remand home.

Initially, the organisation of pastoral care at Greenfield had confirmed his worst suspicions. These had been aroused by the apparently endless succession of disaffected young teenagers who had passed through the children's homes at which he had worked. If any one thing characterised these children it was their failure at and dislike of school. If one thing characterised the school reports which were invariably forwarded by the Juvenile Courts, it seemed to be the teachers' dislike of and ignorance about these children. Keith had qualified as a teacher partly to escape from the antisocial hours of residential staff, but mainly because he had become thoroughly disillusioned with a system of residential care which in theory existed for the benefit of deprived children, but in practice existed as a sop to public conscience and could be relied on only to create greater problems than it received.

Originally, he had intended to serve an apprenticeship of two years at a comprehensive school, and then seek a post in a day special school for maladjusted or ESN(M) children. The informal invitation to the year tutor vacancy surprised him. He knew Henry Price, the school's deputy head, and responsible for all welfare, pastoral care and discipline matters, well enough to realise that he usually got what he wanted, and played for time. "Why are you suggesting this to me?" he asked, "You know I haven't always seen eye to eye with you on pastoral care – in spite of my lengthy teaching experience!"

"It's your lengthy teaching experience that makes me think you've got time to learn", Henry replied mildly. "Yes, but what if I learn the wrong things and come to the wrong conclusions?" "In that case, I shall look forward to some fascinating discussions!" replied Henry.

Keith went ahead and applied, mainly because he had already started to doubt his critical assessment of the school's pastoral care structure. Apart from a small sixth form there were 1,000 pupils, mainly drawn from two large council estates and some older, smaller type of owner-occupied houses. The catchment area lacked the lower and the upper 25 per cent limits on the economic continuum, Keith had once heard the head of maths say in justification of his department's rather poor exam results.

Pastoral care was co-ordinated by year tutors, each of whom was answerable directly to Henry Price. Their job was to lead a team of class teachers, each of whom stayed with the same class from admission until the final year of compulsory schooling. The year tutors were discouraged from seeing children themselves except as a holding operation in an emergency. Similarly, they were expected to direct all enquiries and complaints about a child to his class teacher. Parents had learnt that they should ask for the class teacher if they were worried about their child's progress, and would only be passed on to someone else if he couldn't answer their particular query. Each class teacher was expected to meet every child's parents at least once a year, through a home visit if they did not turn up to open evenings. In addition, everyone who accepted a class teacher's post realised that he would be expected to teach his class for their first two years in the school, and take them on a residential week to the school farm in the second year. Year tutors were brought in only when the system seemed to be falling down with some child. When they were brought in, their job was to identify why the school was failing with the child, not to discover something in the child or his family which could explain why he was failing in the school.

The school had no unit or sanctuary for pupils with problems, and with the head's full support Henry Price made clear that he would never countenance one. His arguments were:

(i) problems are created by the school's organisation, not by children; for example, if you stream or set dull or difficult children into a bottom class, it is no use complaining if they learn dull or difficult patterns of learning or behaviour;

(ii) the strongest pro-social pressure group is the conforming, achieving majority of pupils in a well-organised, mixed-ability class; removing the most difficult pupils from this pressure group is doubly damaging, both by enabling them to react adversely on each other, and by removing them from pressure to conform;

(iii) a behavioural unit or sanctuary reduces the class and subject teachers' commitment to teach the school's least successful pupils, and reduces the need for senior staff to look critically at the school's own organisation and teaching in order to discover ways it may exacerbate the problem;

(iv) there is no way in which one or two teachers responsible for a unit can provide the range of curriculum activities that all parents should expect from a comprehensive school;

(v) segregating problem children is as illogical in a comprehensive system as skimming off the grammar school cream.

Keith Evans' reservations about the pastoral care structure had been prompted by the apparent concern about school organisation at the expense of understanding the individual child and his family. He now accepted that this initial assessment was unfair. Teachers at Greenfield School spent a lot of time talking both to children and to their parents. The fact that the purpose of the interviews was to improve the child's performance at school did not prevent teachers from learning a lot about the children as individuals and about their families. Looking back on his social work career, Keith now felt strongly that he and the social workers in the field had spent far too long taking social histories which at best were totally irrelevant to the problems facing the child or his family, and at worst a gross invasion of privacy. At Greenfield School, teachers might ask about the child's behaviour at home; similarly they might ask if the parents could think of anything that might have unsettled him, but only if this would help them to know why he was failing to make progress or behaving in a difficult way. The approach was at the same time more limited and more constructive.

He was less happy about another aspect of the system. The high level of pastoral care expected from class teachers led inevitably to a wide range of quality. Some class teachers tackled the job enthusiastically, imaginatively and conscientiously. Others seemed to regard it as a tedious chore. There was no provision for a child to change class teachers since this struck at the heart of the school's mixed-ability organisation. Thus children with a lazy class teacher were stuck with that teacher for their whole career. Similarly, class teachers and children who clashed were stuck with each other. It was no answer for Henry Price to say that there were always more teachers who wanted to take a class than there were classes. Admittedly he did from time to time urge one of the less satisfactory class teachers to accept "promotion" into responsibility for some administrative chore, but this did not altogether overcome the problem.

When he tackled Henry on this after his appointment as year tutor, the reply was unsympathetic, "If class teachers are falling down, it's the year tutor's job to raise the standard − that's what we pay you a scale 3 allowance for!" Later though, he gave a more thoughtful reply. School organisation, he argued, was a compromise between the needs of the majority and those of the minority. Any system in which the latter dominated the former had something radically wrong with it and should be altered. The school might not cater for some children very well, and the reason might well lie partly in the class teachers.

Finding a way to help an individual, or even a group of individuals was not particularly difficult; the challenge lay in finding a solution which did not create worse problems than the ones it cured. Keith himself would never have been appointed a year tutor if it were not thought that he could deal with the school's most troublesome pupils more effectively than most of the class teachers. Yet if year tutors did start dealing with these pupils themselves there would be a snowball effect, "and the last state of that house shall be worse than the first", concluded Henry sententiously.

The same arguments naturally applied to Keith's other major reservation, namely the school's policy against any form of behavioural unit. Both as a

154

residential social worker and as a student completing his graduate certificate in education he had visited special units in ordinary secondary schools. He had liked the atmosphere in most of them, and been impressed by the teachers' concern for and knowledge of the children. On the other hand, he had to admit that many of Henry Price's criticisms seemed to be justified. With only one exception all the unit teachers were vague about their success in returning children to ordinary classes; the only exception was a unit where the teacher's role seemed to be limited to child minding, as all work was set by the child's regular teachers.

Keith knew that if he accepted the year tutor post he would need at least two years to make a success of it, and this might mean giving up his plan to enter special education unless he was willing to accept a drop in salary at a time when his family would most need the money. Paradoxically, his decision to stay at Greenfield was based on the fact that the school had referred no children for special education for three years. "Which seems to suggest", he observed to his wife, "that most of the children who end up in schools for the ESN(M) and the maladjusted go there because of the system in their referring schools rather than because of any personal difficulties peculiar to themselves."

Questions

1 Keith Evans had come to some pretty depressing conclusions about secondary schools during his years in residential social work. How might the schools defend themselves? Why are school reports for the courts or for the social services department so often inadequate?

2 Why do you think Keith Evans regarded provision of residential care as a sop to public conscience? How could it create worse problems than it began with?

3 What are the practical difficulties of the same form tutor staying with his class until they reach school leaving age?

4 Has the school got the emphasis right, in expecting year tutors "to identify why the school was failing with the child, not to discover something in the child or his family which could explain why he was failing in the school"?

5 What are the possible dangers – and strengths – in this approach?

6 Henry Price gave five arguments against behavioural units. Are they valid? How would you answer each one?

7 From what you know of a social worker's approach, do you agree with Keith Evans' strictures on their activities?

8 Henry Price saw it as the year tutor's job to raise the standard of class teachers. As a year tutor, how would you set about this?

9 Do you agree with Henry Price's view that year tutors should be able to deal with problems more effectively than form tutors, but that it would be counter-productive for them to do so?

10 How could a unit be organised to ensure that the majority of pupils *did* return to the mainstream of the school?

11 In your experience, have children been referred to special schools as much because of the system in their previous schools as because of their own personal problems?

Andrew

Main themes

1 The most effective expression of disapproval at antisocial behaviour is from other pupils rather than from teachers.

2 As a sanction, exclusion can only be effective if it is seldom used.

3 One function of pastoral care is to provide a compromise between the needs of children and those of teachers.

Keith Evans was in the middle of a social studies lesson with a class of first year children when an older girl came in and gave him a note. "Please come to my office at once, H.P." After hurriedly setting his class some work, he went down to Henry Price's office to find the head, Henry, and a third year boy, Andrew O'Hagan there. Andrew looked deflated, sullen; Henry unusually sharp and formal. The room smelt strongly of drink. "We've a problem, Mr Evans. This young man is to be excluded from school pending discussion about his future education between myself, the headmaster and his parents. Please will you take him home and give his parents this letter. Come straight back and see me on your return. I have already spoken to his father on the telephone and he will be expecting you."

Keith put Andrew, unprotesting and obviously drunk, in the back of his car and checked that the child lock was in operation; he did not want to arrive at the O'Hagans' without Andrew. On the way he asked, "What's all this about then, Andrew?" trying unsuccessfully to sound casual. "That bloody 'erbert insulted me", muttered Andrew, "so I wrapped a chair round her ugly face!" The tone discouraged further questions, and in any case they were nearly at the O'Hagans' house. Still wondering vaguely who "that bloody 'erbert" was, Keith let Andrew out of his car as Mrs O'Hagan came bursting out of the front door, berating Andrew and demanding to know whether Miss Hibbert had recovered. Excusing himself hastily, Keith returned to school.

On Keith's return Henry Price had recovered his composure. "You know that Andrew was absent this morning. It appears that he and a seventeen-year-old friend spent the morning knocking off in Woolworths; then they spent lunch-time drinking a bottle of whisky from a supermarket. After lunch they separated and Andrew thought it was time to pay a visit to the Alma Mater."

"Monica Hibbert noticed at once that he had been drinking and told him to wait outside the classroom before she took the register. He refused, so she sensibly told him to sit down quietly and sent another boy to find me. Meanwhile, Andrew had produced a packet of chewing gum and started offering it around. It appears that the others tried to stop him, and when he pushed one of them off his chair Monica told him he was in a disgusting state and making a fool of himself. He retaliated by picking up a chair and threatening her with it, just as I came in. Actually, I'm fairly sure that he only tried to hit her because he saw that I was close enough to stop him but it was quite an unpleasant moment all the same. I marched him straight down to the head and then looked after him while the head rang his parents. Apparently they thought he'd been at school all morning. That was where you came in."

"Where do we go from here?" asked Keith. "Is Monica all right?" Miss Hibbert, it appeared, was shaken, but had insisted on taking her normal lessons for the rest of the day. The matter would be reported to the Chief Education Officer and chairman of the school governors. Henry and the head had decided to allow a week for Andrew and his parents to worry about the likely repercussions of the day's events, and for the police to make inquiries about the thefts from shops. After this "cooling off" period, the O'Hagans would be invited to visit the school to discuss their son's future. If both he and they seemed suitably penitent, the school would consider under what circumstances Andrew might be able to rejoin the fold.

Five days later a detective sergeant in the local police told Henry informally that he believed the juvenile liaison squad were preferring charges. Andrew, however, had never been in court before, so it was safe to assume that he would not be removed from home, let alone from Greenfield School as a result. A note from Mr O'Hagan expressed his apology for what had happened and hoped that Andrew would not be expelled for good. Monica Hibbert was urged by her union, the National Association of Schoolmasters/Union of Women Teachers, to sue Andrew for assault. This suggestion was eventually dropped, partly because she regarded the assault as somewhat technical, partly because she thought the resulting publicity would reflect badly on the school as a whole, and partly because she did not really regard Andrew as totally beyond the pale.

To be honest, Monica Hibbert was not one of the more enthusiastic advocates of the class teacher system, and she had twice before let herself become involved in confrontations with children, though neither as serious as the present one. On the other hand, both her teaching and her pastoral care duties as a class teacher were always carried out reliably and conscientiously. Two days after the incident she told Henry Price that she hoped Andrew would return to her class if and when he returned to school.

Andrew's return was in fact already under discussion. The first stage of this was for Henry Price and Keith to review his educational progress and behaviour since admission to the school. In the normal way Monica would also have been involved, but Henry had decided that the particular circumstances required a higher level discussion. By no stretch of the imagination could Andrew have been called a model pupil, yet he had not until now caused anyone exceptional concern. His attainments were considerably below average, but he was thought to be working only slightly below his potential. He tended to mix with the least desirable elements, but until now had not been in trouble with the police. Education had never seemed to be the family's highest priority, yet nor had his parents been particularly hostile or even unhelpful towards the school.

Thus, the school's willingness in principle to re-admit Andrew was not in doubt. The important question was not whether to re-admit, but how. At all costs, Henry said, Andrew must be prevented from appearing as any kind of a hero; it was equally crucial that the other pupils should recognise the seriousness of the incident. "I hardly think that's likely to be a problem", objected Keith. "If we asked the rest of his class they would all say don't re-admit him at all." Henry knew this was true, but also thought it would be wrong to re-admit Andrew as if nothing had happened.

"We could put him in a different class", said Keith. "They all know that never happens, so it would cause quite a stir. The trouble is that it might undermine Monica, and create the impression that she has rejected or can't cope with Andrew, neither of which is true." Their eventual decision was both prosaic and logical. By the time he returned Andrew would have missed at least ten days school. He must catch up the work he had missed. As his exclusion resulted from misbehaviour in the lunch hour, he must spend every lunch hour and break in the library, except when actually eating his meal, until he had completed all the work he had missed. With careful arrangement Keith reckoned that this would keep Andrew out of circulation for the rest of term.

The next stage was for Monica to inform her class of Andrew's possible return. "I understand", she told them, "that Andrew O'Hagan and his parents have asked if he may return to school. The headmaster is considering their request, but I have told him that I personally have no objection. If he does return, I hope you will just accept his presence, and in particular that you will not ask him endless questions about his stupid behaviour ten days ago." There were a few murmurs that Andrew did not deserve to be allowed back, but by now the incident, if not forgotten, was no longer fresh in the pupils' minds.

The head and Henry Price saw the O'Hagans and Andrew on their own. They found they had no need to impress either on the boy or his parents the seriousness of their position. Apart from everything else, police charges were pending. With a show of reluctance, the head teacher said, "In view of what you say I am prepared to ask his class teacher if she is willing to accept his apology and agree to me offering him one last chance in the school on the conditions I have outlined; but I must make quite clear to you that if she says no I will back her to the hilt."

As previously arranged, Monica came to the head's office in answer to his telephone call and listened patiently while he repeated his conditions for Andrew's return, including the lunchtime work. She then accepted his apology and suggested to her colleagues that he should go immediately to his history lesson, after which he should come straight to her classroom to collect his work for the lunch hour.

"That", said Henry Price complacently a week later to Keith Evans, "was an object lesson in the management of a potential crisis. Andrew O'Hagan was the

158

first pupil we've excluded for two years. He and his parents were absolutely horrified. Now, if we excluded as frequently as certain nearby schools, which shall remain nameless, parents would no longer treat it so seriously and a successful return to school would be correspondingly more difficult to arrange."

Questions

1 When pupils were excluded from schools in which you have taught, how was this carried out? Were the pupils sent home on their own, or taken home? Were their parents notified in advance?

2 Was the procedure employed in excluding Andrew consistent with the school's need to maintain discipline and the parents' need for information about their child's exclusion and the circumstances surrounding it?

3 In what other ways might Monica Hibbert have handled the situation that led to Andrew's exclusion? Is there anything you would criticise about her actions?

4 What is the school's legal position in excluding a pupil? What is the authority's? If the child is not to be formally and indefinitely suspended from school, is it legally permissible to insist on a "cooling off" period during which the child receives no education?

5 Monica Hibbert asked that Andrew should return to her class. Would you agree to this request if you had responsibility for the decision?

6 "The school's willingness in principle to re-admit Andrew was not in doubt". Should it have been?

7 What is the likely outcome of Andrew's court appearance, bearing in mind that the shoplifting was his first known offence?

8 If asked, the other pupils would have been against Andrew's re-admission. How might their critical attitude have been used constructively in his re-habilitation?

9 If the school used corporal punishment, would it have been effective for an offence like Andrew's? If not, why not?

10 Do you think the arrangements for Andrew's return were as satisfactory as possible? How might they have been improved?

11 The head's interview with Andrew's parents was obviously "stage-managed". Effectively?

12 Do you agree with Henry Price's conclusions in the last paragraph?

Further Reading

The following list is by no means exhaustive. The intention is simply to provide suggestions for the reader who wishes to pursue some of the themes developed in the case histories.

Counselling and pastoral care

Black, D. (1974) What happens to bereaved children?, *Therapeutic Education*, (Spring).

Cowmeadow, P. and Elliott, F. (1975) Sexuality and violence as defences against the pain of death and rejection, *Therapeutic Education* **3** (i).

Goldacre, P. (1978) Work with bereaved boys in a secondary school, *Therapeutic Education*, **6** (ii) 26−7.

Holden, A. (1971) *Counselling in Secondary Schools*, Constable.

Jones, A. (1970) *Counselling in Practice*, Ward Lock Educational: London.

Marland, M. (1974) *Pastoral Care*, Heinemann: London.

Rogers, C. (1951) *Client-centred Therapy*, Houghton-Mifflin.

Rose, G. and Marshall, T. F. (1974) *Counselling and School Social Work*, Wiley: Chichester.

Spooner, R. (1979) Pastoral care and the myth of never-ending toil, *Education*, (2nd March) 251−2.

Taylor, H. J. (1971) *School Counselling*, Macmillan: London.

Reading

Bugler, J. (1976) Janet and John for the high jump, *The Guardian*, (30th January).

Cashdan, A. and Pumfrey, P. D. (1969) Some effects of the remedial teaching of reading, *Educ. Res.*, **11**, 138−42.

Daniels, J. C. and Diack, H. (1958) *The Standard Reading Tests*, Chatto and Windus: London.

Department of Education and Science (1976) *A Language for Life* (The Bullock Report), HMSO: London.

Gilliland, J. (1972) *Readability*, Hodder and Stoughton: London.

Lawrence, D. (1973) *Improved Reading Through Counselling*, Ward Lock Educational: London.

Pumfrey, P. D. (1976) *Reading: Tests and Assessment Techniques*, Hodder and Stoughton: London.

Schonell, F. J. and Goodacre, E. (1974) *The Psychology and Teaching of Reading*, Oliver and Boyd: Edinburgh.

Yule, W., Rutter, M., Berger, M. and Thompson, J. (1974) Over- and under-achievement in reading: distribution in the general population, *Br. J. Educ. Psych.* **44**, 1–12.

Support services

Department of Education and Science (1978) *Special Educational Needs* (The Warnock Report), HMSO: London.

Fitzherbert, K. (1977) *Child Care Services and the Teacher*, Maurice Temple Smith: London.

Gillham, W. (ed.) (1978) *Reconstructing Educational Psychology*, Croom-Helm: London.

Local Government Training Board (1972) *The Role and Training of Education Welfare Officers*, Dept. of Education and Science: London.

Terry, J. (1976) *Social Work and the Law: a guide to the Children's Act, 1975*, Sweet and Maxwell: London.

Teacher—pupil interaction (including behavioural approaches)

Blackham, G. J. and Silberman, A. (1971) *Modification of Child Behaviour*, Wadsworth: Belmont.

Cicourel, A. V. and Kitsuse, J. I. (1971) The social organisation of the high school and deviant adolescent careers, in Cosin, B. R., Dale, I. R., Esland, G. M., MacKinnon, D. and Swift, D. F. (eds), *School and Society: A sociological reader*, Routledge and Kegan Paul, in association with the Open University: London.

Galloway, D. M. (1977) Application of behavioural analysis and behaviour modification in school psychological practice, *Bull. Br. Assoc. Behav. Psychother.* **5**, 63–6.

Hargreaves, D. (1967) *Social Relationships in a Secondary School*, Routledge and Kegan Paul: London.

Hargreaves, D., Hestor, S. K. and Mellor, F. J. (1975) *Deviance in Classrooms*, Routledge and Kegan Paul: London.

O'Leary, K. D., and O'Leary, S. G. (eds) (1972) *Classroom Management*, Pergamon: New York.

Remedial education

Cashdan, A. and Pumfrey, P. D. (1969) Some effects of the remedial teaching of reading, *Educ. Res.* **11**, 138–42.

Chisholm, B. J. (1977) Remedial help within non-streaming, *Forum for the Discussion of New Trends in Education* **20**, 24−6.

Cleugh, M. F. (1957) *The Slow Learner*, Methuen: London.

Goodwin, C. (1974) Leicestershire: Countesthorpe College, *Remedial Education* **9**, 16−18.

Griffin, D. (1978) *Slow-learners: a break in the circle*, Woburn: London.

Lytton, H. (1967) Follow-up of an experiment in selection for remedial education, *Br. J. Educ. Psych.* **37**, 1−9.

Sampson, O. C. (1975) *Remedial Education*, Routledge and Kegan Paul: London.

Special Education (including special groups in ordinary schools)

Anon. (1979) How children's special needs are "ascertained", *Where* **148**, 156−8.

Boxall, M. (1973) Nurture groups, *Concern* **13**, 9−11.

Cleugh, M. F. (1957) *The Slow Learner*, Methuen: London.

Coard, B. (1971) *How the West Indian Child is Made Educationally Sub-Normal in the British School System*, New Beacon Books: London.

Department of Education and Science (1978) *Special Educational Needs* (The Warnock Report), HMSO: London.

Department of Education and Science (1978) *Behavioural Units*, HMSO: London.

Dunn, L. M. (1968) Special education for the mildly retarded − is much of it justifiable?, *Exceptional Children* **35**, 5−22; reprinted in W. G. Becker (ed.) *An Empirical Basis for Change in Education*, Science Res. Associates: Henley-on-Thames.

Galloway, D. M. and Goodwin, C. (1979) *Educating Slow-Learning and Maladjusted Children: Integration or Segregation?*, Longman: London.

Gorrell-Barnes, G. (1973) Work with nurture-group parents, *Concern* **13**, 13−16.

Jones, N. (1973) Special adjustment units in comprehensive schools: I Needs and resources. II Structure and function, *Therapeutic Education* **1** (no. 2), 23−31.

Jones, N. (1974) Special adjustment units in comprehensive schools: III Selection of children, *Therapeutic Education* **2**, (no. 2), 21−6.

Laslett, R. (1977) *Educating Maladjusted Children*, Crosby Lockwood Staples: London.

Osterling, O. (1967) *The Efficacy of Special Education*, Scandinavian Univ. Books: Uppsala.

Rowan, P. (1976) Short-term sanctuary, *Times Ed. Supp.* (2nd April), 21−4.

Wills, W. D. (1971) *Spare the Child*, Penguin Books: Harmondsworth.

School attendance

Galloway, D. M. (1976) Size of school, socio-economic hardship, suspension rates and persistent unjustified absence from school, *Br. J. Educ. Psych.* **46**, 40−7.

Hersov, L. (1960) Refusal to go to school, *Journal of Child Psychol. Psychiat.* **1**, 137–45.

Hersov, L. and Berg, I. (eds) (1980) *Out of School*, Wiley: London.

Kahn, J. H. and Nursten, J. P. (1968) *Unwillingly to School*, Pergamon: Oxford.

Reynolds, D. and Murgatroyd, S. (1977) The sociology of schooling and the absent pupil: the school as a factor in the generation of truancy, in H. C. M. Carroll (ed.) *Absenteeism in South Wales: studies of pupils, their homes and their secondary schools*, University College, Faculty of Education: Swansea.

Tennent, T. G. (1970) The use of section 40 of the Education Act by the London Juvenile Courts, *Br. J. Criminology* **9**, 175–80.

Tyerman, M. J. (1968) *Truancy*, Univ. of London Press: London.

General

Barnes, D. (1976) *From Communication to Curriculum*, Penguin: Harmondsworth.

Clegg, A. and Megson, B. (1968) *Children in Distress*, Penguin: Harmondsworth.

Department of Education and Science and the Welsh Office (1977) *A New Partnership for Our Schools* (The Taylor Report), HMSO: London.

Jennings, A. (ed.) (1969) *Discipline in Primary and Secondary Schools*, Ward Lock Educational: London.

Jones-Davies, C. and Cave, R. G. (eds) (1976) *The Disruptive Pupil in the Secondary School*, Ward Lock Educational: London.

Kamin, L. J. (1977) *The Science and Politics of I.Q.*, Penguin Education: Harmondsworth.

Lindsay, C. (1970) *School and Community*, Pergamon: Oxford.

Marland, M. (1970) *Head of Department*, Heinemann: London.

Martin, N., Williams, P., Wilding, J., Hemmings, S. and Medway, P. (1976) *Understanding Children Talking*, Penguin: Harmondsworth.

Maurer, A. (1974) Corporal punishment, *American Psychologist* **29** (no. 8), 614–26.

Pinkerton, P. (1974) *Childhood Disorder: a psychosomatic approach*, Crosby Lockwood Staples: London.

Rosenthal, R. and Jacobsen, L. (1968) *Pygmalion in the Classroom*, Holt, Rinehart and Winston: Eastbourne.

Rutter, M. (1967) A children's behaviour questionnaire for completion by teachers: preliminary findings, *J. Child Psychol. Psychiat.* **8**, 1–11.

Rutter, M. (1972) *Maternal Deprivation Re-assessed*, Penguin: Harmondsworth.

Rutter, M. (1975) *Helping Troubled Children*, Penguin: Harmondsworth.

Rutter, M. (1978) Family, area and school influences in the genesis of conduct disorders, in Hersov, L., Berger, M. and Schaffer, D. (eds) *Aggression and Anti-Social Behaviour in Childhood and Adolescence*, Pergamon: Oxford.

Rutter, M., Maughan, B., Mortimore, P., Ouston, J. and Smith, A. (1979) *Fifteen Thousand Hours: secondary schools and their effects on children*, Open Books: London.

Stott, D. H. (1973) *The Social Adjustment of Children* (2nd edn), Univ. of London Press: London.

Tough, J. (1976) *Listening to Children Talking*, Ward Lock Educational: London.

Wedge, P. and Prosser, H. (1973) *Born to Fail*, Arrow Books: London.

Index

courses, 5; in grammar school, 130–1; rejected, 113; remedial teaching by, 23–4, 27–8; *see also* pastoral care

Croft House Primary School, 53–60

curriculum: mixed ability, 95–8; remedial, 86–90; stagnation, 137

cutback, staffing, 21–4

Daniels and Diack's Standard Reading Tests, 30, 63

Dean Valley Primary School, 37–43

death, 18, 124–7

delinquency *see* disruptive behaviour; police

depressed area, school in, 45–52

desertion, 65–6; *see also* death

dilemma of counselling and pastoral care, 5–8

disapproval, pupils', 156–9

discipline, 35, 82, 84, 95–8

dislike for child, 25–8, 57–8

disruptive behaviour: and bereavement, 124–7; and insecurity, 140–3; in primary schools, 26, 35, 65–6, 73–6, 81–4; in secondary schools, 113–14, 116, 124–7, 140–3, 157–9; after withdrawal, 74–6; *see also* legal action

doctors, school, 53–4, 74, 76, 147; *see also* health

Doris Henley Primary School, 29–36

economic restrictions, 21–4

Education Act (1944), 65, 67, 101, 108

education social workers *see* education welfare officers

education welfare officers (e.w.o.), 5; in primary schools, 15, 53–6, 58–9; in secondary schools, 108–11, 121, 123, 141, 143, 148–51

educationally sub-normal *see* ESN

Elden County Junior School, 21–8

epilepsy, 81, 84

Equal Opportunities Board, 106

ESN schools, 5–6, 57–60, 67; *see also* special schools

e.w.o. *see* education welfare officers

examinations, external, 87, 128–9, 131

exclusion as sanction, 156–9

expectation, teacher, 45–8

family: and absenteeism, 49–52; disorganised, 34; knowledge of, 152–5; 'normal', 7' and poor progress, 17–20; stress, 3–8, 17–20, 25–8, 41–4, 81–3, 91–4, 149–51; *see also* parents

Family Service Units, 5

flats, children from, 18, 105

forgetfulness, 26

form tutors, 152–5; *see also* class teachers

Galloway, D.M., 5–6, 8, 10, 161–2

Gillham, W., 6, 10, 161

girls, punishment of, 103–7, 125

Goodwin, C., 5–6, 10, 162

grammar school, 128–35

grandparents, 27, 124–7

Greensfield Comprehensive School, 152–9

group tests, 30, 63; *see also* tests

Grove Bank Comprehensive School, 136–43

guilt, 26, 28, 135

haemophilia, 38–40

handicapped children, 21, 24

Hargreaves, D., 8, 10

health problems: children's, 21, 24, 38–44, 49–52, 73, 91–3, 144; parents' 17, 27, 42, 58; siblings', 81–4

hearing tests, 18–20

Henry Beardsley C. of E. Comprehensive School, 120–7

Hill Top Primary School, 69–76

home *see* family

home-school liaison, inadequate, 13–16

home teaching, 125–7, 143

home visiting, 15, 55, 58–9

illness *see* health

inequality, 13

insecurity, 140–3

reward for attendance, 35
Reynolds, D., 5, 11, 163
rewards, 35
risk, children at, 46, 48
rocking, 66, 68
Rogerian therapy, 135
Rose, G., 6, 11, 160
Rutter B(2) scale, 70, 72
Rutter, M., 5, 11, 161, 163

Sampson, O.C., 6, 11, 162
sanctions *see* punishment
sanctuary *see* behavioural unit
Schonell's Graded Word Reading Test,
   61–2; *see also* tests
secondary schools, 86–159
self-confidence, need for, 118–19
senility, 27
sibling relationships, 81–4, 93–4,
   134–5
social services, 17–20, 33–6, 53–6,
   109–11; *see also* education welfare
   officers
Southlands Secondary School, 103–11
special schools, 5–7, 22, 46, 57–60,
   65–8, 102
Special Schools Removal Officer, 4
specific learning difficulties, 88, 90
Spooner, R., 3–4, 11, 160
stability and curriculum stagnation, 137
stammering, 91–3
status quo, as obstacle to change, 45–8
stealing, 33–5
Stonerace Infants School, 77–84
streaming, 128, 131, 153
stress *see* family
success, need for, 83
Supervision Order, 34, 36, 109
support services, 6–9, 53–6; *see also*
   social services
suspension, 124, 127
Syncrofax machine, 118
system, beating the, 108–11

Taylor Report, 104
teachers: assault on, 156–9,
   expectations of, 45–8; and support
   services, 53–6; *see also* parents
teaching and pastoral care, 4–5, 140–3

temper problems, 100, 102
tests: attainment, 90; behaviour, 70, 72;
   formal, 65, 67; group, 30, 63;
   hearing, 18–20; intelligence, 25, 28,
   63, 67, 99, 102; reading, 25–7, 30,
   61–4, 91–3
theft, 33–5
'thick class' stigma, 91–3
threat, special school as, 102
toy library, 17–18, 20
truancy: primary school, 8, 33–5,
   49–52; secondary school, 108–11,
   137–40, 143

under-achievement, 43
uniform grant, 148–9
union, teachers', 157
units *see* behavioural units
universities, counselling courses in, 5
unpredictability, 81, 84

violence, parental, 109; *see also*
   corporal punishment

Warnock Report, 5, 7, 15, 22, 24
weakness, organizational, 37–40
Wechsler Intelligence Scale, 67, 99
welfare *see* social services
wetting, 73–6
White Horse Infants School, 13–20
withdrawal groups, 29–32, 77–80, 90
withdrawn behaviour, 73–6, 91–4,
   116–19, 136–9
working-class parents, 13–14, 27,
   112–13, 115

year tutors, 2–3, 152–5
Young's Non-Readers Intelligence
   Test, 25, 28

168